Best wish

VOLUME III

Hollis Baker
&
Alice

These stories originally appeared as a weekly column in the Liberty Hill, Texas newspaper. Some of them may even be true. The reader can decide which ones to believe.

Copyright © 2016

All rights reserved. No part of this book may be copied or reproduced without the written consent of the author except for brief quotes.

PRINTED IN USA

DEDICATION

*This book is dedicated
to those young folks
that did not know
things like this
had ever happened*

and

*to those older folks
that, perhaps, have
forgotten that
it may have happened.*

Acknowledgments

Thanks to my wife Alice for her
encouragement, support,
and suggestions.

Thanks to our son, Greg, for his
editing skills, and strength
to insist I get it correct.

And, thanks to Bob Rook for his
patience, editing skills, and
perseverance
In getting it done

VOLUME III

Hollis Baker

Following Cattle Trails North

This weekend we drove to North Texas to celebrate our great-granddaughter's First Holy Communion. She was beautiful; all dressed up in a white frock, carrying flowers, marching down the aisle to the music of a grand organ playing an ancient hymn. She smiled at the proper times, and didn't miss a step. A fitting pageant to warm a great-grandmother and great-grandfather's heart. She is not the first, nor the last, to be a part of the play, but we know she is the prettiest.

On the drive north I got to thinking about our great-great-grandfathers that had driven that same route north, but for a different reason. Thousands of Longhorn cattle were driven up the environs of U. S. 281 some 150 years ago, on their way to Dodge City and other rail heads. Their troubles on the road made our trip "a walk in the park." The Indians, legally the owners of the land, had been reduced to hungry bands of humanity. Their only resources for food, the buffalo, we wiped out, forcing them into begging for a few cattle. If the hearts of our grandfathers were not softened to sharing, the hungry Indians were forced to steal.

The comfort of just getting through the workday would overwhelm most of us today. Eating meals cooked from a chuck wagon must have been healthy, but questionably enjoyed in comfort. Sleeping arrangements were not what humans had become accustomed to. Sand storms, strong wind, as well as rain, sleet, and hail was a daily challenge.

Perhaps one of the greatest problems on the cattle drive was crossing the streams, often flooding, along the trail. On our trip I began recording the names of creeks, branches, and rivers we crossed easily on bridges. Just out of Liberty Hill flows the North San Gabriel River. Today it flows intermittently, but I am told it once ran full, year-round. Then came a surprising number of creeks, each prone to flooding after a rain. They are; Little Rocky, North Rocky, Mesquite, and Sulfur Creek by the town of Lampasas. After Lampasas came another slew of creeks; Burleson, Lucy, School, Patterson, Simms, then the Lampasas River. The hamlet of Adamsville welcomed us on our drive. I wondered how these creeks and rivers got their names; I fancied they were names of cowboys that got in a fight, got shot, or just for the heck of naming them something. After Adamsville there was only one named stream, Freeman Branch. Why it was named a branch and not a creek remains a mystery. The trail then threads thru the village of Event followed by more creeks; Partridge, Cow House, then the town of Hamilton. Just north of Hamilton flows the Leon River. At Hico someone named the stream Bosque River, an unusual tag for a name of a river in central Texas. Hico claims to be the place Billy the Kid hid out after being chased from the territory that was to become New Mexico. More creeks, branches, and some that I call gullies, followed quickly. Then came the mighty Brazos River. We crossed easily on a steel and concrete structure. Difficult to imagine how the cowboys managed to get thousands of longhorn steers to brave the waters. However; they did.

We drove into Seymour, Texas on time, found Sacred Heart Catholic Church, and enjoyed witnessing Olivia take communion. The folks of Seymour and surrounding towns were warm and most hospitable. I wondered if some of these men and women were the descendants of the strong, adventuress cowboys that drove cattle up the trails. I expect they are.

Stilts

One bright spring day the circus came to our little town. They set up in Mr. Wingren's pasture just at the edge of our village. What an exciting thing it was to watch them raise the big tents and piece together the grandstands. They used the elephants to pull and push and lift things. It was a new world for us boys. We wanted to get real close to the action, but the rough talking working men ran us off with words we had never heard. Some I haven't heard since.

 All the guys and gals working in the circus seemed heroic to me. The strong man was a site to see. He picked up barbells with ease that were marked with big numbers. He even stacked up a dozen or so pretty girls and lifted the whole bunch over his head. The horse wrangler came into the center ring with all kinds of little horses, medium sized horses, as well as big plough horses. They ran in circles, marched to music, and reared up on command. Lions, tigers, and all kinds of jungle animals were exhibited. I sure was glad they were kept in iron cages. I felt the Lion Tamer who got into the cages with those fierce looking animals was not too smart. He had a gun and a whip, but looked puny to me. There were all kinds of acts that filled the big tent. A brass band blared out all kinds of music; hawkers sold popcorn and snow cones. The swinging trapeze act was ok....but us guys swung from Dad's chinaberry tree with calf ropes all the time. They even shot a little man in a red spangled suit from a cannon across the ring. The big gun roared and smoked and he landed in a net, unhurt. We wanted to try that act, but did not know where to find that much gun powder. Lucky us.

But the one that really caught my eye was the tall man. He wore striped pants, a bright star-printed jacket and a stovepipe hat. He looked to me to be 12 feet tall, and I guess he was. Dad explained that the man was wearing stilts. I never heard of that. Dad said, "We will make you a pair."

Early the next morning I scrounged lumber from the barn and Dad got his carpenter tools from the garage. "Here, son, you saw a while, I am tired." I liked being an active part of the building. "We are going to make you and your sister, Leta Mae, the best set of stilts you ever saw." And he did.

We could hardly wait to try walking, high in the air, maybe 12 inches up, where we could see the whole world and all that is in it. The learning curve to use the stilts was steep. A few scraped knees, scratched elbows, and smashed noses convinced us to rest a bit.

Mom got in the act too. She found two old cans of paint sitting on a shelf and painted the stilts; Leta's were red and mine green. That's the year we had a circus anytime we stepped onto the stilts.

Danger Hiding in the Grass

Yesterday's late spring rain was a beautiful thing to experience. It was a pleasant surprise. Greg, our son the gardener, was planting tomato seeds in pots for our fall garden. The sky was bright blue with a few scattered fluffy clouds. Then the clouds began to gather and way in the distance came the music of thunder. A hasty retreat to the porch was followed by a quick, heavy downpour of an inch of rain; insurance for a green summer and a full, productive garden. The trees, bushes, and pasture grass were all putting on new leaves and all was well. Except for one small thing.

Chiggers. They are bright orange. And the grasses are teaming with them. Walk to the mail box and you are sure to attract a body full of the rascals. They seem to congregate around the ankles, groins, and belt line. In a short time the itching begins. Scratching feels so good, but does not help. In fact I fear it makes the itch worse. The big boys at the pool hall have all kinds of suggested cures for the pests. Nail polish, applied to the red welt is a popular thought. That really does not help. Applying any kind of ointment, such as Vaseline, skin cream, calamine lotion gives one the hope of relief. All of this doctoring may give temporary relief, but not much else. The itch continues. Grandma used to tell us that what we ate made our bodies attract chiggers. I don't know about that. She laced most of her cooking with a heavy dose of garlic. I am not sure that helped keep the chiggers at bay. I know it will keep friends and family at a distance. The girl cousins and aunts used less perfume in the summer time. They said the good smell attracted the pests. Perhaps it did.

I went to my book shelf and retrieved from my set of Funk and Wagnall the volume 'C' to find more information. The big book said chiggers are the early stage of the adult arachnid "chiggerious." That didn't help much. Further reading said the pupa stage was irritating but did not infect the body with a secondary problem. Only the itch remained. That is the biggest understatement of the season. The book did not even make any suggestions for relief. I returned the book to the shelf with a mental note that the information was lacking in any kind of help.

I returned to the pool hall for another dose of their wisdom. Most of the sagacious crew had some idea for help. They were unanimous in the fact that too many baths would attract chiggers. I kind of liked that idea. I could tell, standing downwind from them, they all embraced that thought. Tobacco, red meat, and whiskey were mentioned, but I did not put much faith in that defense. One quiet fellow sitting in a dark corner of the hall had a good suggestion. "Just tie a kerosene soaked rag around your ankle. It will keep the fellows away," he said. They all agreed with him.

From all this scientific study I have come to three solutions; don't take too many baths, use plenty of kerosene, and scratch all you want.

Driving Around the Town Square

Out in the pasture sat an old car body. The wheels were long gone, the windshield had been busted out by them mean ole boys, and the paint rusted away. But to us kids it was still a shiny, brand new car. Often we all piled into the ragged seats and played like we were driving to town. We added the sounds we felt the car made in driving down the road..."*varoom, bam bam, moova,*

moova." The horn made a pleasant sound as we passed imagined other cars..."*ugah ugah*." Sometimes the horn went, "*beep beep"* or *"honk honk".* They always moved over for us in our hurry. Donald Hicks usually grabbed the steering wheel and was in charge of the adventure. When he suddenly yelled ..."*screech, screech,"* we knew he had slammed the brakes on, turned around, and headed back to home..."We forgot our lunch money." Donald was good at supplying the sound effects of our trip. Did not matter to us that we had not moved an inch in that meadow. We all laughed and went along with the imagined trip to town.

We abandoned the old car trips when we got our first bicycle. We had the same adventure we had had in the old stripped down car, only we moved. We covered the town on our bikes. We were able to visit the cotton gin, with all its sounds and excitement, then check the temperature of the water in the creek. We peddled to the top of the hill east of town just to see who could coast the farthest. The winner got the honor of "Best Coaster." That meant a lot to us. In the heat of summer, we got the idea that the wheel bearings needed servicing. Some of us had New Departure rear wheel bearings, and some of us had Marrow systems. Whichever one you had, you just knew it was the best. We greased everything we thought might need it, including our trousers, shirts and hands.

Then a city guy, Jerry Daugherty, moved to our town. He brought an innovation to our bike riding. Jerry took playing cards, bent them around the fender supports and fastened them with his mother's clothespins. Flipping the spokes it made a sound that we fancied was just like a motorcycle; *"Putter, putter, putter."* Sounded to us kids just like a big Harley Davidson bike 'Cadalacking' around the town square. Now get a half dozen bikes, all equipped with cards flipping, and it was pure pleasure.

Then came our first car. The wheels were there, the windscreen intact, and not too much rust showing; we felt grown up. We drove around our town during the day, hoping the girls were watching. But late at night, some of the boys had to see how long a line of rubber he could lay. It was fun until Wallace Riddle, our sheriff, suggested we put a stop to that sport. Most of us stopped, except Jerry. He was the champion of laying rubber, until Sheriff Wallace let him spend the rest of the night in the jail. We gave him the crown of "Rubber Laying" but he eased off the action also.

Now sometimes, going to the store or Sunday church, I remember making those sounds, hearing the puttering of flipping cards, kicking up gravel, and laying rubber, with all the sound effects, I am a kid again. That is until Alice suggests I have passed the age of pretending. I guess she is right...but just saying "VARROOM!!! VARROOM!!!" makes me feel good.

Old Man and Dog Picking Flowers

I don't know how old the man was. He didn't walk around our block...he more like shuffled around our block. And his little dog shuffled a step or two just behind the man. They were the same age-old. The two of them even looked alike. Both were grey. Not the color of grey, just no color. There was no suggestion of a past occupation of the pair; cowboy, rough-neck, teacher? The old man's clothes hung on his little body more than fitted it. In cold weather the old man dressed the dog in a dog wrap, and even it was grey. The dog, and the old man, did not seem to be enjoying shuffling down our street. It seemed it was more their duty. Every morning about good daylight you could expect to see them easing along, in no hurry, just going down the street. They were there in most weather, hot and dry or wet and cold. Windy? Sure. And on those beautiful spring mornings? Of course! Often he held in his little hand a small bunch of spring flowers pulled from an empty lot. In winter his bouquet often was some dry weeds.

We lived on a corner lot in a small wooden house surrounded by a meager lawn that I enjoyed keeping mowed and trimmed. A few shrubs that city folks called landscaping dotted the lot.

"What you need," Alice suggested "is some color in the yard. Why don't you plant some flowers somewhere"? I didn't like the thought of digging, fertilizing, planting, and watering but duty is duty.

"Where do you suggest I put a 'spot' of color?"

"Out by the curb, of course," she said. So I dug. I raked the thin soil. I went into the country and got a pick-up load of rich dirt to add to the bed. There, that should do the job, I thought. I planted my mother's favorite flower, zinnias. Each day I hurried home to inspect the bed for action. Soon little green plants pushed through the soil and I knew we were on the road to 'color' success. And they grew. Soon buds began to show. A bit of color. But the flower bed did not burst into a grand show of color. I grew tired of being disappointed so I just ignored the flower bed. They were on their own.

Next weekend I got up early to work the yard. The old man and his dog were halfway down the street shuffling toward home with a hand full of my flower blossoms. A flash of anger swept through my body and I started to yell at the old man. But something stopped me. I was dumb founded. Later that day I grumbled to some of my neighbors about the old man. "Don't you know what he is doing?" "Yeah, he is stealing my flowers," I said. "Don't you know the old man's problem?" Of course in my haste of life I didn't. "The old man's wife is bedridden and is not expected to live much longer. Each day he exercises his dog and looks for something to take her to brighten her life. Your bed of flowers is a perfect answer to his quest."

I looked for a hole to hide in. My selfishness overwhelmed me. Here was an opportunity for me to be a partner in bringing a bit of color into the lives of two fellow humans, and a dog. I had almost destroyed that chance to be a part of the magic of love.

One seldom has an opportunity to grab the 'golden ring'.

The zinnias out did themselves. The blossoms **burst into the full color** of the rainbow. They produced more flowers than the old man needed. I noticed he only took a few each day, and the plants doubled their blooming. That gave me a great feeling of giving. Perhaps it eased my hurried chase for more stuff.

Then I noticed I had not seen the old man and his dog in a week or so. I asked the neighbors about him. "Didn't you hear? His wife died, and he moved to live with his daughter in another city."

The zinnias continued to bloom gloriously. But there was a bit of loneliness about the 'spot of color.'

Brittney Gets to Meet John Steel

"Hey, Pa, I want to meet John Steel," our granddaughter Brittney said. "I hear you talk about him and I've never met him. He sounds interesting."

"Well, Britt, I haven't seen John in a while," I said. "I guess we could drive out there Saturday and see if he's home."

Saturday morning came bright and clear. I sure was glad to have Britt with me when it came to opening John's wire gate. Britt jumped out and almost tore the gate off the post getting it opened. "Pa, you need to make Mr. Steel a decent gate. That thing almost bit me while I was opening it," I drove through without answering her suggestion. I have plenty to do without that aggravation.

We bumped up John's rocky road to his house. Sure enough, that spotted dog met us with plenty of bark and a mean growl. I had not seen that dog so agitated. With a stick from my pick-up I convinced him to go under the porch.

I hollered "Hey John, you got company!" No answer. That was strange. I knew he was home. His pick-up was parked under the big shin oak tree in the yard, "Hey John," I hollered. All was quiet from the house. His milk cow was still in the pen and was bawling for her calf. The calf answered with a weak bleat. That did not look good.

We walked up on the wooden porch and I banged on the door, "Hey John, you in there? I brought my granddaughter Britt to meet you." A weak voice said, "Come in."

We went in. There John lay in a tumbled bed. His right foot propped up on a pillow, all red and swollen. His face was pale and it was easy to see he had a fever and had been there some time. "John, what happened to you?"

"Well, if you must know," he whispered, "A couple of nights ago I stumbled on that blasted porch and got a splinter in the ball of my foot. I can't get it out." Our granddaughter, who is a registered nurse, took one look at John and said, "I'm calling EMS."

John rose up on one elbow and said, "Don't you dare call them guys. I ain't going nowhere in a truck with lights flashing and sirens blasting."

Britt kept dialing her cell phone. "You better just put that phone down. He won't go" I said. "Let's see what we can do."

Britt commanded me to put a pan of water on to heat, got an Ibuprofen from her purse and, in no uncertain words, told him to take it. John took the pill. I brought the hot, soapy pan of water and set it by the bed. Britt told John to sit up and put his foot in the water. "No. It hurts," John said.

Brittney, with fire in those blue eyes said, "Now, Mr. Steel, you either soak that foot or I am going to call EMS."

"Well, I ain't going to do either one."

Brittney got in his face and said "JOHN STEEL, SIT UP, AND PUT YOUR FOOT IN THAT PAN OF WATER." John sat up and put his foot in the pan of water. I introduced Brittney to John. "I think she is a keeper

Baker," he said with a weak grin. I agreed with that.

I knew John was now in good hands and would be up soon. I went to the barn, let the cow out, watered the hogs, fed the chickens, and turned the wind mill off. By the time I got back to the house I could hear John telling Britt stories of running around the world working the rough-neck game. He told Britt of drilling for oil in the Philippines, West Texas and Venezuela. I had already heard all those stories so I sat in John's rocker on the porch and tried to make up to that spotted dog. He wasn't having much of it. Britt and John laughed and talked for some time. They seemed to be getting along as if they had been friends a long time. "John, I will be back out in the morning to check on you. You do what the nurse told you to do, you hear?" He grumbled something. On the way home Britt said, "Pa, I sure enjoyed meeting your friend. You take good care of him."

Making Hay While the Sun Shines

This year the spring rains came, and kept coming, giving us the greenest land in a few years. The flowers burst forth with a grand show of color. The blues, oranges, and pinks outdid themselves, painting the hillsides and valleys. The trees of the woods breathed a sigh of relief and grew tall. Even the bushes and underbrush bristled with eager growth. The meadows became a vibrant sight with a covering of grasses. And the grass grew. Soon the pasture grass looked more like a field of planted grain. It even waved with the gentle winds of early summer. Me and my blue grass-eating riding lawn mower worked at keeping all the acres neatly cut and trimmed. And the grass grew.

It was a valiant effort. The mower gave out in sheer exhaustion. I got my tools and worked on repairing my faithful blue baby. I soon learned that you "never send a boy to do a man's job," fit me to an uncomfortable 'Tee'. I could not repair the mower. Our son Greg came to my rescue and hauled the sick cutter to the repair shop. The repair man found the problem, and ordered the part. The part came in a few weeks. And the grass grew. He repaired the mower and it sure cut well - for a few days. Back to the shop. New part ordered and the machine repaired...again. In the meantime the grass just kept on growing. I must say the mower tried to keep up, but alas, the task was too much. By now, in the 100 degree heat of summer, the grass had grown knee high.

Then out of the blue came our neighbor, Darwin Wiggers riding his shining green John Deer farm tractor pulling a shredder. To me he looked like a Knight in Shining Armor, riding a prancing white stallion coming to save a man in distress. Or, perhaps he looked more like Matt Dillion and John Wayne rolled into one with guns blazing. I wish you could have seen the culprits scatter from the Long Branch Saloon. In just a few hours Darwin had the meadow cut. With a tip of his hat and a subtle wave he rode off into the setting sun.

Now I had a pasture covered in about a foot of mowed grass. I raked grass. I piled grass. I soon found I could use the Blue Cutter to push the grass into mounds. The meadow now looked strange with mountains of grass. Now what to do with the Alps of grass? I found that by lowering the deck of the mower to the lowest setting it was easy to push the mounds around the base of the surrounding trees. I think the trees will enjoy the comfort of shaded feet. This is, 'a work in progress', for the Alps loom large. I work each morning while it is cool, and life is a joy. Surely I will master the task.

The fellow who said, "Make hay while the sun shines," was not from Central Texas. Not with a smile on his face anyway. Well, perhaps if he had a neighbor like Darwin Wiggers he could muster a slight grin.

Great Grandpa Ulysses S. McCoy

I knew Grandma was getting tired of great-grandpa Ulysses' visit when she told me to get him out of her kitchen. "Take him on the porch and get him busy telling more of those wild stories of his."

It wasn't hard to get him telling stories, but getting him to leave Grandma's kitchen was a little harder doing. We practically had to drag him onto the gallery and set him down in his rocking chair.

"Tell us about Little Billy, Grandpa. What happened to him?" we asked.

"Little Billy? I don't know about a Little Billy..."

"Oh yes you do, Grandpa. Remember telling us about going on that last cattle drive, and you rode lead and the cowboys rode point and flank and Little Billy had to ride drag at the rear of all the cows? You had all the cowboys stuff cotton in their ears. And him getting lost in Shamrock. And you said you never saw him again," we said.

"Oh, you mean that Billy. Little Billy Simmons. We picked him up on the trail about Lampasas. Well, I meant to say we didn't see him again 'till we got way up in Kansas. I didn't worry about him much. I figured he would show up in time to draw his wages, and he did," he said. "A few years later I was up in that country and passed through Shamrock. I asked around about Little Billy and nobody seemed to know who I was talking about. I said his name was William Simmons, from Lampasas County. Now that brought a bright smile to their faces. 'Why you mean our Sheriff, William Simmons. He has just been elected Sheriff of Wheeler County. We all sure like him,' they said."

"So I rode over to Wheeler and found 'Sheriff Little Billy.' He wasn't little any more. He had grown tall and with his flaming red hair made an impressive looking lawman. I asked Sheriff Simmons how he got lost from the herd back in Shamrock that time."

"Well, when you told us to stuff cotton in our ears and keep driving the cows up the trail I decided I wanted to hear what was going on for myself, so I didn't put cotton in my ears. One of those pretty little girls on the sidewalk lured me to go home with her. Wasn't hard for me to make that decision, so I left the herd."

"That pretty little girl was soon my wife, took me to her home, introduced me to her pappy and ma, and begged her dad into letting her keep me. I didn't argue the point, so I soon became a part of the family. Besides her pappy had several sections of ranch land and more cattle than we were driving up the trail," Sheriff Little Billy said.

We asked Great-grandpa Ulysses if that was all there was to the story?

"What story?" Grandpa asked.

"About little Billy," we said.

"Oh. That is about it. Except he made a good sheriff, had a bunch of red headed kids, and became a rich rancher. So you see a little cotton can make a lot of difference in a man's life."

Grandpa dozed off about that time. We left him in the sun on the porch and went to the kitchen and helped Grandma finish making oatmeal cookies.

Cooking Beans for Lions Club

The Lions Club International is involved in many charitable activities. We supply eye exams and glasses, free of charge, in many third world countries, as well as here at home. Also, we provide summer camp opportunities for needy children. Lions Clubs give scholarships to promising students for higher education. We are pleased to have the chance to do this work.

However, being involved in these tasks requires money. That puts the Lions Club in the fund raising business. Here in Liberty Hill we sponsor "Thrill of the Hill" bike race. That race attracts many bikers, from all over the state, that enjoy the challenge and beauty of riding the Central Texas Hill Country. The riders pay for that fun, and the Lions Club earns money for our projects.

Another fund raising activity is the 5-K walk/run race. It has been well attended and all seem to enjoy the challenge. I have not joined in the activity of being in the 5-K race. Maybe when they reduce the distance to 1K I will consider it. Walking around the block might be more appropriate for my physical abilities. However this race does raise moneys to fund the Club's work.

The newest fund raising work is our 'Fish Fry Saturday'. The men and women of our Club do all the work and use the VFW building to cook and serve the food. The folks of our area have been kind in coming to our dinners. Right off you would guess the guys went to the river and caught all those catfish. I hate to tell you that we did not do that. We caught the catfish at HEB. They are all farm raised and are as fresh as if we had camped out on the river bank and caught them ourselves. Maybe we are missing something here. The ladies of our club cook the pies and cakes in their kitchens and bring them to go with the meal.

I was asked to cook a big pot of pinto beans. Right there is where the trouble started. Now I cook the best pinto beans in Central Texas. Everyone agrees to that brag. Of course you know Alice taught me all the skills of cooking beans, but don't go telling that around town. I enjoy the fame of being the best bean cooker around here. The night before the fish fry I soaked five pounds of pinto beans. I also started cooking a beef brisket just to get the juice to flavor the beans. That is one of my secrets to making such good pintos. The next morning I was a bit pushed with other demands and asked Alice to spice the beans. I sat out all the spices on the cabinet for her to use: salt, chili powder, black pepper, red pepper, garlic powder, and cumin. She dutifully did. I came in from my other duties and sampled the beans. They tasted bad. I added a bunch of ketchup. That didn't help. They still tasted awful. I added onion flakes. Bad choice. No improvement. I looked at the spices I had sat out for Alice. All seemed to be in order; salt, pepper, garlic, chili powder. Then the next item....wasn't cumin at all, it was cinnamon. There was the culprit, cinnamon. Cinnamon does not fit pinto beans. It makes a terrible taste. I poured the whole pot out into the dog's dish. One sniff and he turned up his nose and went under the porch.

I looked at the clock. I just had time to force a pot of pintos for the Fish Fry Saturday. I tossed the cinnamon to the back of the cabinet, and got the pot finished in time for our dinner. They were not my champion beans. However not many noticed and I promise to do better next time, if they dare ask.

The University Years

In the early '50s the war was over and all us young men flocked to the Colleges and Universities to earn the advantages of an education. The University of Texas built several complexes of inexpensive housing to serve the crowds of G.I.s flooding the school. Our neighbor was Fred and Ruth Snyder. One morning I saw him busy loading his car.

"Hey Fred. Fred Snyder, where are you going?" I hollered. "I am going fishing with Lonnie Hollingsworth. You want to come along? I think you and Lonnie would get along just fine." I had never met Lonnie until that day. We drove to the lake and started a friendship of fishing and conversation that has lasted more than 60 years. I have noted the conversation has outlasted the fishing by a mile. I guess you could say we were better at park bench sitting than fishing. Lonnie and I have spoken of cabbages and kings from London to Honolulu; with a few sessions at Rockport thrown in for good measure. Together we have solved worldwide pandemics of health, pestilence, and financial disaster. However few, if any, of our suggestions have been embraced by world leaders. Pity. I have always admired Lonnie's business knowledge, his political good sense, and his community service. Our world could profit by more men like Lonnie Hollingsworth.

By the way, that first fishing trip was a grand adventure. Fred caught a few sun perch about finger length while Lonnie and I filled a bucket of smaller ones. Our wives, Nancy and Alice, laughed at our meager haul of fish, but cooked them and set a feast for us of fish and friendship for life.

Mr. Swift Could Roll a Cigarette

My Dad, in his little grocery store, stocked several brands of smoking tobacco. The "ready rolls," like Camels, Lucky Strike, Chesterfields, and Kools, were expected. They sold for 15 cents a pack. The rich folks bought them. The farmers, ranchers, and laborers only bought tobacco that came in neat little tin cans. There were several brands. Prince Albert was the most popular. The cans were built kind of flat, and a size that fit in their overalls pockets. They sold for 10 cents per can. The most popular tobacco came in little cloth sacks, with a yellow drawstring that had a neat round paper tag attached to the drawstring. There were two brands of sack tobacco: Dukes Mixture, and Bull Durham. They sold for five cents a pack. A packet of "papers" was glued to the back of the sack so the smoker could "roll his own."

I remember Mr. Swift's easy way of rolling his cigarette. He would open the sack with one hand while getting a paper with his other hand. He laid a finger of tobacco in the folded paper and rolled it up with that hand, then brought it to his lips and moistened the edge of the paper and completed the roll in one easy motion. With his other hand, he flipped the little tag to his teeth and pulled the sack closed and returned the sack to his pocket. While he pocketed the sack, he extracted a kitchen match. Some men struck the match by pulling it briskly across their pants leg. Not Mr. Swift. In that smooth action of making a cigarette, he lit the match by flicking the head of the match with his thumbnail. The explosive flame lit the cigarette as he flipped the spent matchstick out the door in a cloud of blue smoke. I enjoyed seeing the action. It was a thing of art. We admired Mr. Swift.

Us kids collected the empty tobacco cans for all sorts of uses. The cans made good fishing packs. You could fill the can with string, hooks, sinkers, and corks from medicine bottles. Or sometimes we devised special cans for safety. We stuffed the cans with matches, aspirin, small bottle of iodine, a compass, and always plenty of string. I liked the tobacco sacks best. We used the sacks to carry important things around with us. Frogs and snakes were popular. They really are useful around girls. We were always alert for shiny rocks and shells. They fit well in the sacks.

A story went around, like in most little towns, that if you saved up a 1,000 Bull Durham tags and sent them in, the company would give you a brand new bicycle. We believed the story. A friend's uncle that lived over in Lampasas, said he knew the kid who had done it. Well, that got us busy collecting Bull Durham tobacco tags. I think I saved up to 30 or 40 tags.

That would never get a bicycle in a hundred years. We decided to pool our tags. While we were excited about the pleasure of owing a brand new bicycle, together we saved 197 tags. That dampened our spirit. Besides, summer had arrived and it was time to go swimming.

If you know of a "Mr. Swift," that can roll and smoke a roll-your-own with class, call me. I would like to see that one more time.

Falling in Love with Madam March

The month of March is a mistress dressed in the cloth of irritating anger, seductive promise, and dashed hopes. Foolishly, it is easy to fall in love with the winsome Madam March.

I finally rid myself of February and eagerly embraced the arrival of March. I am like a schoolboy with my first infatuation: giddy, impetuous, silly, excited. March's early days are full of sun-bathed, warm southern breezes, models of her handmaiden Spring.

With abundant joy, I raced to the tool shed, and armed myself with spade, rake, and fork. I turned the cold stubborn soil with abandon. I raked the beds to a beautiful, smooth finish. What I gained was a sweaty shirt and an ache that kept me awake most of the night. The next day I planted broccoli, tomatoes, and peppers. Sure, I knew better. That night we got a cold, hard rain. Dawn brought clear skies and a cold, stiff north wind. The tomatoes and peppers were cold burned, and the broccoli was ravaged by the rabbits. The rain packed the fertile soil solid again. If crying had helped, I would have. My mistress, March, did not even toss me a kiss.

I fear I am not much of a gardener. However, I do have a stubborn streak that runs the length of my aching back. When the cold winds turned, and brought the southern breezes home, I returned to my garden's seductive call. I tilled the soil again. I raked it smooth. I replanted the peppers, tomatoes, and broccoli. To foil the rabbits I installed an electric fence. Now let the little critters touch the wire with their pink noses. And the garden grew. Until the deer found the tender plants. I added two rows of electric fence above the rabbit wire. And replanted again. The warm winds were a wink from my imagined love, Madam March.

Now the dry winds swept the garden. It is amazing how quickly the soil dries to a hard crust. I hoed the dirt. The grass and weeds seemed to enjoy my work. I weeded the garden. I watered the garden. And it grew with a passion. Was this a tossed kiss from my love, March?

I do not think so. If it was, it was a derisive kiss. A lover can be so cruel. The skies grew dark, the lighting flashed and thunder filled the air. An ominous roar foretold of the coming hail. The storm was short lived. The ice-laden clouds seemed to hover over the garden, relishing the destruction of all the plants. But stubbornly I replanted.

Today the garden looks lovely. The peppers, tomatoes, broccoli and other plants are robust, green and bursting with vigor. The promise of the harvest smells sweet. And I think Madam March has fallen for my stubborn ardor.

Confusion Has Encompassed These Acres

I am a little confused about the goings on in Washington these days. I am not knowledgeable about political activates in the world, and especially those in our national government. I understand the world is in a financial crisis. Some say it is a Chicken Little sort of thing. Others say, "The end is nigh." The word 'sequester' is being bandied about, and that only adds to my confusion. I would look it up on this computer, but I don't know how. What does that word, sequester mean? I decided to go visit John Steel, and his old spotted dog. Perhaps they could enlighten me.

As I parked my battered pick-up truck at John's house, his dog gave me a few half-hearted barks and a meaningless growl and retreated beneath the porch. A lot of help he is going to be I thought. John hollered from the comfort of his rocking chair on the front porch, "Come on in, Baker. I just made a new pot of coffee." Now, to John, new coffee means he just added another scoop of grounds to yesterday's brew he had not drank and boiled it again. But I did not dare refuse his offer.

I quickly got to the reason for my visit. "John, what is the meaning of the word sequester?"

"Sequester" he replied, "means 'to put away, alone, in a secluded place." That did not help me at all.

"I mean, like they are talking about in Washington."

"Well, in that way, it means, the note is due and it is time to pay the loan."

"How much is the note?"

"Thirteen trillion dollars," John replied.

That astounded me. "Why don't we just pay it?" I asked.

"Can't," he said. I still didn't understand. "Show me," I demanded.

John got his skinny frame out of his rocker, ambled into the yard. He picked up a stick that had fallen from a Spanish oak tree and began scratching numbers in the dirt. He scratched $13,000,000,000,000.00, and a division sign behind it. "How many folks are living in the United States?" he asked. I said about 600,000,000. I was surprised I knew the number. John scratched out zeros from the big number and the little number. He turned to me and said, "$25,555.00."

"What does that mean?" I asked.

"Every man, women, and child in the United States of America owe a little over 25 thousand dollars to the treasury." My head spun, I had to sit down. I couldn't pay that much money. Alice can't pay that much. What if we were like some of our neighbors, with two children; they would owe a $100,000.00 dollars to avoid total collapse.

"John, how did we get into this mess?"

"Well, let me explain that by asking you what you make a month?"

"$50.00," I replied.

"No, I mean when you had an honest job!" I told John I made about $20,000.00 a year. "Now," he continued," what if you spent $20,001.00 per year?"

I would be one dollar in the hole I said.

"Right. That is what we have all been doing. Especially the government." "And I fear that is exactly what the world has been doing."

I drove slowly back home. I almost stopped at the Exxon for a coke. No, I decided. That thing cost $1.07. Can't afford that.

Sometimes Get Rich Quick Schemes Fail

At the coffee shop a few days ago, where us old guys hang out, Gary Spivey brought me a check. It was from Bastrop Hide & Fur Co., dealers in Furs, Pecans, and Produce. It is a bit yellowed, and is number 406. It lists C. P. Cloud as owner and Joe Spivey as manager. Joe Spivey was Gary's grandfather.

Today it is hard to believe we had traffic in wild fur-bearing animals. This check has a date of 1930 printed on it. I haven't seen a lady wearing a fur coat since some time in the '50s. However, up until quite recently a fur coat was a sign of success. I remember wanting to buy Alice a mink jacket, but she had to settle for rabbit. She looked spiffy in that rabbit jacket, and I played as if it was mink. She wore that thing, with pride, until most of the hair had fallen out. Alice did not comment, one way or the other. Today she wears cotton, or rayon, and still looks spiffy.

I must admit, I trapped for fur during the winter months when the hides were supposed to be at their prime. I had a trap line about a mile long. I bated those dozen traps with sardines, old pieces of bacon, or anything that smelled to high heaven. Running my trap line on those frosty cold mornings was a grand adventure. I just knew each morning that I would find a mink or at least a coon in one of my traps. Alas, that never happened. My total catch was one grey rat, three possums, two skunks, and a crow. And that was over a period of years. Possums and skunks sold for a nickel each, but there was not a market for rats or crows. All those years I fancied I would get rich soon if I could catch enough animals. I think the animals were pleased when I quit trapping and looked for honest work.

Of course, that check is not filled out or signed. Gary did not say why. I guess I didn't meet his deadline. What I did find interesting was the list of pelts they wanted to buy. Printed on the check were skunk, possum, and ringtail. I suppose these were the cheap hides, and most numerous. The list goes on: coon, civit cat, lynx, wolf, badger, and mink. I don't think I ever saw any of these animals in the wild, and I know none were brought into the buyers at my hometown. Muskrat and fox finish the list. Except for one: house cat. I cannot remember any of the old timers talking about trapping, skinning, and selling a house cat pelt. Wouldn't Alice look pretty wearing a calico cat jacket?

If the market for house cats ever opens up again, I could become rich overnight. However, I don't think I am going there. I do not care what Gary's grandfather wants. However, Gary did buy my coffee that morning. Thanks.

Wartime Airplane

During the World War II years us kids spent much of our time reading about the fighter planes. We were all excited talking about the different kinds. We knew all about the P-40 fighter plane. We learned its looks, what it was powered with, how many guns it carried, and how fast it could fly. As new ones poured from the factories, we added that information to our knowledge. We built balsa wood models that were supposed to fly, powered with rubber bands. They rarely did. Except they did fly in our minds. And we were the handsome, fearless pilots. Our constant dream was of the day when we would be able to fly our own airplane.

Walking home from school each day was drudgery. On hot days, we hated carrying our jackets. If it was a cold day, we wished we had a thicker coat. Walking up the hill to my Dad and Mom's store seemed more than I could manage. Dad's store had groceries, and two gasoline pumps. The wide driveway invited customers to stop by for service. I could see the store about 200 yards away. As I came into sight of the store I could see something unusual parked in the driveway. No, it could not be what I thought I saw. It looked just like an Army airplane. It was olive green with a big Army Air Corps symbol painted on its side.

I began running up the hill. Sure enough, it was an Army airplane. It wasn't a P-40, or a

P-51 - it was a Piper Cub. My excited mind raced, looking for a reason an Army plane, any kind, was parking in our driveway. Maybe Dad had bought one for me to play in. I knew that could not happen. Perhaps my rich uncle had landed there. Unlikely. As I reached home, I was exhausted from the running and the excitement. *It was a real Army airplane, a reconnaissance plane used to spot enemy positions.* And there, standing beside the plane, was a brave, handsome pilot, about 18 years old. I wanted to run up to the Piper and touch it, look inside the cockpit, and stand close. A subtle wag of the pilot's finger warned me to stand back. I ran into the store to ask Dad what the Army's airplane was doing in our driveway. Dad said the pilot noticed he was low on fuel, had spotted our gasoline pumps, so he landed on the highway then taxied into our place. He needed 100 octane gasoline. Unfortunately, we only had 90 octane. While the pilot guarded his plane, Dad called around town and found a station that had the higher octane fuel. Mom took a five gallon gas can and brought back the fuel.

By this time, Sheriff Riddle drove up with his siren blaring, and his lights flashing. He helped the pilot fuel the tank, then drove up the highway to stop approaching cars. The pilot turned to us, gave us a snappy salute, climbed into his handsome steed and roared up the highway in a perfect take off. We never knew where he was from, or where he was going. But for a moment I had a real live Army Air Corps airplane that I could touch.

Impetuous Youth in the Dating Game

Young men some times act a little foolish when dating. I guess it is in our genetic make up. I like to think that is what causes some of our dumb actions. I know it is not our intellect.

The first time I saw her she was still in pig tails and pinafore dresses. Fact is, I didn't see her. She was just my buddies little sister, and in the way of our important pursuit of life.

The next time I saw her she didn't look like the same little girl. In fact she wasn't the same little girl. That coal black hair had been cut and styled. She had grown tall, slender, and with a smile that would make a gawky boy run out to the rail fence and stand on his head. That was what I did. I could tell right off she cared little for the Tom Sawyer type.

She did agree to go on a picnic as my date. I don't give up easily. I thought, I will impress her this time for sure. I climbed a tall rock bluff that skirted the creek. Half way up I looked down and there she was, climbing that bluff like a professional.

Next time we were together I changed tactics. I talked of books I had just read. Well, I had read the titles. I mentioned far off places I had been. And I talked of cabbages and kings and wondrous things. Yes, she knew the authors. Had been to the far off places, and met the Cabbages and Kings and his Queen.

On our next date we went swimming at the lake. I jumped off the dam into the water 20 feet below. She did an Ester Williams swan dive. Hardly rippled the water. So far I was batting zero in the impressing game. You would have thought I would have learned something. I didn't.

I know, I thought. I will take her to dinner at some swell restaurant in the big city. I spent almost ten dollars on dinner, held her while she danced. Then she introduced me to the mate-tre-de, who was a close friend of the family. I slunk back to the car. Trumped again.

OK. I decided to try the Tom Sawyer tactic one more time. Our town had a water tower. It must have been two hundred feet tall. There was a ladder I managed to reach. I started climbing with my devil may care attitude. I was scared stiff. I should have know better than to use that old trick again. Looking down, here she came: a step at a time with ease. We walked around the water tank on the inspection walkway. There was a ladder that went up to the top of the tank. I had come this far, I might as well go for it all. I climbed to that little steel ball that sat atop the water tank. She climbed to the top also. There we sat on the ladder, holding the little steel ball, while I prayed Sherriff Riddel was deep asleep. From this height we could see to the end of the earth, and all that was in it. With my pocket knife I scratched our names on the ball: Hollis + Alice. Thin air and youth makes a boy do things he would be afraid to try on firm ground. I summoned my last bit of courage, called upon my eloquent use of the English language, and said "You wouldn't want to get married would you?"

She whispered yes. We were married. And we have been climbing towers, bluffs, and swimming lakes ever since.

A Letter from Cousin Jim McCoy

Dear Hollis:

I was just thinking about a big game hunt I once had with Cousin Richard. In the summer of my 11th year we hit the road north. We were visiting my mom's family in Colorado. There were no Interstate highways in those days and the average speed limit on any of the various routes was around 50 MPH. The thump, thump, thump of the expansion joints in the concrete pavement made sleeping easy. Dad usually tried to leave home around 4 am. That got us to our destination about seven or eight in the evening. We didn't make very good time but we did manage to enjoy the trip.

Richard was a year older than I was and we had always been close, so I naturally got to stay with him and his parents. As we drew near Richard's home I noticed something I hadn't seen on previous trips. There were cotton-tailed rabbits everywhere. When I say everywhere, I mean you would have been hard pressed to find a ten-foot patch of ground that did not have at least one rabbit on it. His parents said they didn't know why there were so many rabbits. His mom said she would be glad to cook a couple of them for breakfast if we would catch and clean them.

Richard and I took that as an easy challenge. We figured that we could just stand in one spot and grab the first one that came within reach. We soon discovered that they were not that dumb. They would not come anywhere close. We changed our tactics. One of us would stay still and the other would try to scare a rabbit close enough to grab. Again, the rabbits were smarter than we were. We changed tactics several times after that. We tried making a net with a feed sack and a broom handle but could not get that to stay together long enough to try it. We tried hitting them with rocks and sticks and various other thrown objects. No danger of either of us making a living as a baseball pitcher. After spending the whole day as abject failures, we slept soundly but vowed not to give up.

The next morning, well rested, we took up the challenge with renewed vigor. We noticed a pile of old brush and logs where rabbits often took shelter. It was not large but they would disappear into one hole then reappear from another. We had no idea how many rabbits or how much space there was under the pile of wood. After a while, we decided to check it out more closely. I lay down, looked into one of the holes, and could not see anything. That is when I really got brave and reached my arm into the opening. I felt nothing rabbity but could tell there wasn't much room. We then really focused on getting the critters to go into the pile so we could see where they came out. We soon detected there were really only two holes the rabbits used. After one entered one side, it wasn't long before he came out the other side. Aaha, we thought in unison. Plugging the exit hole, we put our new plan into motion. Then began the task of herding a rabbit into the other hole. This took a while but we were ultimately successful. Then Richard ran up and stuck his foot into the entrance hole, thus trapping the rabbit. Then we realized we had another problem - how to get the rabbit out. We decided I would get down and reach in as soon as he moved his foot. I was really hoping to grab the bunny by the rear end rather than the front. Eureka, it worked! Soon I had a wiggling bunny by his hind legs. We borrowed my aunt's kitchen knife and made short work of cleaning that one. Again, we were chasing rabbits toward that woodpile and I guess the practice must have helped as the second one worked out easier. With two rabbits cleaned and in the refrigerator, we began to anticipate breakfast the next morning. That breakfast of fried rabbit, biscuits, and gravy was the best I have ever had. I suppose all the work we put into it helped our appetites as well as honing our hunter-gatherer skills.

There were more big game hunts in later years but none that gave me as many fond memories. I now think of Richard each time I see a rabbit cross the road.

John Yarbrough

Liberty Hill lost a great man a few days ago, John Yarbrough. John was a bundle of interesting personalities. When I saw John at church, I knew I was in for some sort of ribbing. John, speaking about my column, would say something like, "Well, you got close. Better luck next week." John's words were accompanied with a broad smile and gentle hug. I did try harder after that. John was a fence builder. I asked him if he ran a crew of men in his business. "No. Just Jose and me. He doesn't speak English and I don't speak Spanish." I found later that John Yarbrough was one of Texas' biggest and best men in the fence building trade. And he could speak Spanish.

John's interests lay in three areas: Church, Sharing, and Fencing. And in that order. John loved his church. If there was a need, he saw that it was taken care of. He felt the older folks needed a place of worship in the traditional way. He bought the old First Baptist Church building and gave it to

Fellowship Baptist Church. I said, "Goodness, John that is a lot of money." John said, "Money is just printed paper. It is no good for anything except helping folks." And that is the way John felt. "Money really belongs to the Lord, and he just loans it to us for a time."

John and his wife Diane, lived on a beautiful ranch out County Road 288. From that front porch, you can see to the end of the world. John loved horses. He sometimes had a dozen or so on the ranch. He said he kept them for the kids and grandkids. I think John just liked horses. He was pleased that horses attract kids. He kept them well fed and they always looked sleek, both the kids and the horses.

I asked John how many children he and Diane had. He looked me in the eye and said 33. I was astounded. He added he and Diane worked with foster children for many years. They adopted many of them. I had the pleasure of meeting some of their children as well as some of the grandchildren. John had a way with the kids. He loved them all and gave most of them different names than their parents had. If one of them looked like a rose, John named her Rose. The kids loved it. Their daughter, Rebecca, met Scott, who was also in the Air Force, in Korea. She brought him home to meet her Mom and Dad. John told Scott, "If you want our Rebecca you will have to beat me in a game of pool". Scott beat him. He got his prize.

Their daughter Melinda was out of collage for the summer. John drove by her house early one morning and said to her, "Let's go." Melinda said where they went was to a fencing job. They worked all day. She said "It was a long day. I met a grand-daughter, Amie, from Houston".

She said everyone loved her grandpa. John and Diane liked to travel in their motor home. On a sudden whim, John and Diane took their granddaughter Sarah on a motor trip to Alaska.

Lana, their youngest daughter, said her dad was a great disciplinarian but in a gentle sort of way. She worked with John for many years. Some say she is as good a fence builder as John was. In fact, Lana and her husband are in the fencing business today.

Their son Wade tells a story of an adventure he had with John and their motor home. They were visiting the Space Center in Florida. John bought a new lighter for his pipe. He filled the lighter with fluid in the living area of the motor home. He spilled some fuel on his hands, pant leg, and carpet. John ignited the lighter. The lighter caught flame, his hands were aflame as well as his pant leg and carpet. It was touch and go for a moment there, but they stomped the flame out. Diane cleaned up the mess.

John spent 65 years fencing most everything in Texas. I expect if God needs any fence work done in heaven he now has the best man for the job.

Watering Grandma's Flower Garden

When you got up this morning, did you take a shower? Brush your teeth? Make coffee? Most of us did. Where did the water come from? From the water faucet, you say.

Where did it go when you were finished using it? Into the sewer probably.

Our grandmothers had a little different water system in their lives. Here in central Texas most farm homes got their water from a well. Some wells were hand dug and were only about 20 to 30 feet deep. To get the water from the well Grandpa sat two posts over the well. About head high he installed a cross board from one post to the other one. In the middle of the cross board he fastened a pulley that held a rope with a bucket tied to the end. To get the water he then lowered the bucket into the well, and pulled the water to the surface with the rope. He then carried the filled bucket to the kitchen. A few trips to the well and back to the kitchen supplied Grandma with the days water needs. Except Saturdays. That was the weekly bath day. Then it took many more trips to the well and back.

Some wells were deeper and had to be bored by a well digger with his big equipment. This kind of well required a different kind of bucket and a lot more rope. This system was used for the horses, cows, and chickens. It worked fine.

Many farms and ranches that were close to a creek or lake used a different method of watering the home. Grandpa searched the place until he found a forked trunk in a tree, shaped like the letter 'Y'. The 'Y' needed to be about five feet long. He then nailed boards across the forked end of the 'Y'. This became his sled for hauling water from the creek to the house in two wooden barrels. One day Grandpa asked, "Think you can haul us two barrels of water from the creek?" "Sure," I quickly replied. However, inside of my little body I was not that confident. I went to the pasture, got Pacer, our draft horse, and harnessed him to the empty sled. "Giddyup I commanded." Pacer did not move. I repeated the command. Again Pacer did not move. I inspected the harnessing. Sure enough, the horse was smarter than I was. I had the collar on upside down. I didn't spill the water barrels but twice getting them to the house. I was kind of proud of myself, having completed a man's job with few errors. Now we could carry a bucket of water from the barrels to the kitchen with ease.

With all the work of getting the water to the house Grandma was not about to just toss it out. She used the water from the dishpan and bathtub to water her yard flowers. And her yard was ablaze with color. She had zinnias, bachelor buttons, larkspurs, holly hocks, and petunias. No one left the place without a big bouquet of flowers.

So tomorrow morning when you shower and shave, thank these modern days for the ease of our water system.

Now That is Getting a Close Shave

Do you remember these road signs?

WITHIN THIS VALE
OF TOIL AND SIN
YOUR HEAD GROWS BALD
BUT NOT YOUR CHIN
Burma Shave

Driving across the country 70 years ago, it was a delight to read the roadside signs advertising Burma Shave. The company made a shaving cream you just wiped on your face. No need to use a brush to make it foam, just shave the whiskers away. The signs were painted white on red, and each line of the catchy saying on a separate board, nailed to fence post. If Dad was driving too fast, we urged him to slow down so we could read the saying. It always brought a smile, and a warm fuzzy feeling. And obviously sold a lot of brushless shaving cream.

> THE BEARDED DEVIL
> IS FORCED TO DWELL
> IN THE ONLY PLACE
> WHERE THEY DON'T SELL
> Burma Shave

Mom, my sisters, and I made a game of seeing who could spot the next sign first. Dad always won. Of course, that raised a good-natured row. "That is not fair," we argued. However that was a part of the game, and Burma Shave knew it. The Burma Shave company boomed after introducing the sign advertising. The company used that advertising method from 1925 until 1963, when Phillip Morris Tobacco bought the company. They decided to abandon the use of the roadside signs.

Many of the signs stressed safe driving. I suspect there were many lives saved with the humorous verses.

TRAIN APPROACHING
WHISTLE SQUEALING
STOP AND AVOID
THAT RUNDOWN FEELING
Burma Shave

How about this one:

HARDLY A DRIVER
IS NOW ALIVE
WHO PASSED ON A HILL
AT 75
Burma Shave

The last of the signs are now in some kids room, nailed to the wall. The Smithsonian has a collection of signs for the future folks to marvel about. Higher road speeds contributed to the demise of the catchy signs. Wider roadways nailed the door shut for the effectiveness of that type of advertising.

There were hundreds of slogans used in the advertising of Burma Shave. The company offered a $100.00 prize for any suggestions that were used. They received thousands of offerings. The company had to hire people to go through the stacks of letters.

Well, all the Burma Shave signs are gone. But those red and white signs gracing our roadsides were a pleasure to read. Perhaps my favorite is:

> WHEN PASSING SCHOOL HOUSES
> TAKE IT SLOW
> LET THE LITTLE
> SHAVERS GROW
> Burma Shave

Wet Tobacco and Sticky Candy is a Treat

We all knew he had a problem. His usual good nature had turned sour, and nothing pleased him. Normally Grandpa Riley was full of stories of Indian fights, adventures with outlaws, and other dangerous encounters. He laughed at the older folks that didn't put much stock in the truth of his tails. But I believed them all. I was pleased when he gave me 25 cents on the sly, and asked me to help him with his favorite bad habit. "I want two plugs of Brown Mule chewing tobacco and you can buy some peppermint candy with the change. I think you can make it to town and back before the rain," he said

The cloud in the northwest sky brought on darkness sooner than normal that day in early August.

I jumped at the chance to help Grandpa and have a little adventure myself. I sneaked to the barn, saddled Pacer and got to town before the rain came. Pacer was known to be a little jumpy in bad weather. I figured, being Grandpa's favorite, I could handle her.

I bought Grandpa's tobacco and my candy just as the rain began. By the time, I got out of town, darkness embraced Pacer and me. We were soon soaked to the skin, but I figured the horse knew her way home and the safety of the barn. As the fury of the storm increased, with lighting and strong winds, I could tell Pacer was getting a little skittish. Half way across Rocky Creek a bolt of lightning struck a giant pecan tree on the creek bank, splintering it from top to bottom. Pacer jumped, bucked me off and ran into the darkness, leaving me dumped in the water. I hollered to Pacer, but to no avail. She was gone. I was totally wet from shoes to hat. Worst thing was the sack of tobacco and candy was floating down the creek. By the flash of the lightning, I managed to catch our precious sack of absolute human necessities.

I didn't remember the fork in the road ahead. The rain was pouring down and the flashing of lightning made things look different. I took the left fork in the road. Sloshing ahead it was soon evident I had made the wrong decision at the fork. I retraced my path, took the right fork, and soon was able to see a light in Mom's kitchen window.

I took my chastisement from Mom and Dad with a little helpful defense from Grandpa Riley. They demanded I unsaddle Pacer and feed her before I could have any supper. Well, I reckoned, that is the way of adventures.

I handed the soggy sack of tobacco and peppermint candy to Grandpa. We all had a great laugh at the thought of him chewing wet tobacco. I did not mind a bit eating sticky candy.

Summer Swimming at Plymouth Hole

One late summer day I decided to take our kids swimming. Our town did not have a pool for us to use, and the local creeks were dry. But I knew where there was a pool that purported to have never dried up. I filled my old "Yellow Dog truck," with our children, Gordon, Jeannette, and Greg. We crowded the cab with sweaty bodies and off-key singing. A fun day lay ahead.

On the way to the swimming hole I told them about the pool's pristine beauty, the deep clear waters and the tall bluff with a water fall. They were eager to see this swimming hole and enjoy the beauty of the place. During our drive I painted verbal pictures of its natural beauty. North Morgan Creek meanders through solid rock canyon walls for several miles. Its banks are crowded with sycamore and willow trees, shading the creek. Above the canyon walls, the cedar brakes peek over the edge, keeping vigilance on the creek bottom. They were eager to see the place for themselves. "How much farther is it Daddy?" "Not much," I offered. However to a kid "not much" can be a long way.

The paved road soon gave way to a dusty dirt drive. Through a gate or two the road turned into a trail that crossed, back and forth, across North Morgan. A side canyon the locals named "Wolf Holler" broke through the canyon's rock walls. We parked our truck at the mouth of the much smaller stream emptying into North Morgan. I found a path that took us up into the cedar brakes. I wanted them to see the pool from above. Summer makes the stands of cedar hot and dry. The climb up the mountain was not a pleasant stroll. Between the thick cedars were stands of brush. It seemed they all had cat claw thorns which snagged our arms and shirts.

We came to the Wolf Holler Creek about a hundred yards above Plymouth Hole. The kids were surprised at how small the stream was. "This little creek can't fill much of a swimming hole," they cried almost in unison. "You will see," I said.

Me and the youngsters splashed down the creek with glee. It sure beat the hot, dry cedar brakes we were in most of the morning. We then broke through the thick shrubbery lining the banks. The kids stopped just a yard from a 20 foot bluff that exposed Plymouth Hole below. They stood in awe at the sight. The little stream leaped free from the creek bed and splashed into a large, clear, pool of water, probably 12 or 14 feet deep. The sun splattered the sight with broken shafts of light, giving the pool the look of a jewel. We made our way down the side bluff and leaped, with a shout, into the water. And we leaped out just as quickly. The water was cold on our hot bodies.

"Spring fed stream," I explained. Our bodies soon acclimatized to the temperature of the pool. We swam, splashed, laughed, and embraced the beauty of nature. Some of the older kids climbed back up the bluff to dive into the pool. Looking down, from above, they decided perhaps a jump into the pool was a wiser choice. I agreed.

The drive home was a lot quieter than the drive in. In fact, they all fell into an exhausted, but happy sleep.

Lyndon B. Johnson's Cowboy Hat

Paul Curtis and a bunch of us guys have coffee almost every Thursday morning at the Hobo Depot Café. I wear a western hat and on occasions, Paul does. We kid each other about our "All boots and hat but no cows," status in life. In a rash moment Paul said, "I have a hat I don't wear anymore, and I am going to just give it to you." Now that suited me fine.

Next Thursday Paul brought the hat to coffee. Hooboy! You talk about a good-looking hat! This hat is a grey Beaver-Deluxe hat from Shudde Brothers of Houston. This hat company has been in business for over a hundred years. They have made hats for stars like John Wayne, Gene Autry, Tom Mix, Dr. Red Duke and a long list of other notables. Now I have one. However, there is a lot more to this hat than meets the eye. This hat used to belong to Lyndon B. Johnson, while he was our President. Now it hangs on my hat rack, in a prominent place in the living room. When I am wearing this hat, I do have a bit of a problem passing a mirror without stealing a glance. There are not many things a Texan wears that make him walk more proud than a good-looking western felt hat. You can have a pair of handmade boots, a big silver belt buckle, and pearl-buttoned shirt, but without the hat, it doesn't quite cut it.

I started to stretch the truth a wee bit, and tell you that Lyndon came to our sign shop and ordered campaign signs for his next election. I was going to say that he was so pleased with our service he took his hat off and gave it to me. I also thought about telling you that one windy day in D. C. his hat blew off, I chased it down, and in thanks, he gave me his hat. Several other stories come to mind, but perhaps we need not go there. That is not what happened. Far be it for me to stretch the truth...that much.

During the '60s, Darrel Royal coached the University of Texas football squads. He made winners of the University of Texas football gladiators during those years. In fact, they mopped the field with the blood, sweat and tears of most of the Southwestern Conference teams. During that time, Royal and his men won the National College Football Championship...several times.

Of course, President Johnson was proud of his home state's winning football record. To show his approval and congratulations, Lyndon sent each member of the coaching staff a Shudde Western felt hat. The men, of course, were pleased and wore them with pride. Pat Patterson, of Liberty Hill, was on that coaching staff. Perhaps Pat was not into western wear, or his wife did not like it, so he gave the hat to Paul Curtis. Then Paul, after getting a new one, gave me the Lyndon hat.

So, now I wear President Johnson's hat with pride. I even sneak a peek at mirrors with abandon these days with no shame. As far as I am concerned L. B. J. gave me this hat. That is my story, and I am sticking to it.

Old Red Brick School Building Reunion

This Saturday, June 1, from one o'clock until dark the class of 1966 will be sponsoring a High School Class Reunion honoring the class of 1963. There were only three seniors in that class; Tony Miranda, James Meyer, and Margie Frazier. However, those three seniors, as a class project, were responsible for getting a modern water system in Liberty Hill. We hope these three seniors are able to attend the reunion, at the VFW hall.

The reunion will have on display pictures, film, and memorabilia of all kind from the "Old Red Brick School Building." Gary Spivey and Billy Ray Guerin have been working hard getting this reunion organized. Gary said the "Old Red Brick School Building" was built in 1928. The building housed all the classes from first grade through the 12th grade. The building served the community well until they tore it down in 1969 to make room for a new high school building at the same location.

The old building housed many outstanding students. W. E. Hines became a college math professor. James Mather, Gilbert Vickers, James Pogue, James Vaughn, Clyde, Cleo, Euel, and Vernon Cox were outstanding football, baseball, and basketball heroes. The last class in the old building, 1969, Mary Parker set a basketball scoring record that still stands unbeaten.

There were other records set that may not be so famous. Three boys spray painted 'freshmen, sophomores, juniors, seniors' on a wall of the gymnasium. No one admitted to the deed. Howard Adair, the school Superintendent, put the school students to work, scrapping, brushing, and sanding the words from the walls. All but three students helped remove the paint. Those three said that to be a part of the cleanup would be admitting to the crime. They were the ones that did the painting. In spite of these acts, the culprits became outstanding citizens of our town.

Troy Joseph told me one Halloween night he and a bunch of boys put old man Riggs buggy on top of the "Old Red Brick School Building." That was some chore when you consider the building was two stories. Then he topped that by saying they put John Fester's pet donkey up there with the buggy. Of course with a little probing they found the culprits. They were made to clean the class rooms until the end of school.

I hope you will have time to go to this reunion. Gary said all are welcome. Invited are those who went to school there, knows someone that went to school there, or anyone who loves Liberty Hill and the "Old Red Brick School House."

Grit: How Sweet It Is

The 20's and 30's were hard times. Especially in the sign business. Local businesses had little money to spend on a new sign for their stores. Many sign men loaded up their pickups with ladders, paint, brushes and all the tools for painting signs and hit the road. We, in the trade, called them "snappers." Their method was to drive across the states looking for an opportunity to "snap up" a sign job that the local sign man had missed. In addition, paying no rent, they often did the jobs for less money. We locals did not like their getting what we called 'our work'. They were a tough bunch of men; however, some were great artisans.

Bill Prince and A. D. Greer were two of the greatest "snappers" I had the chance to meet. They traveled the south and west part of our land snapping signs along the way. If the storeowner did not have the money for a sign, A. D. offered to paint a portrait of his wife or daughter for a few dollars. Somehow, the owner often found money for that. And A. D. was an excellent artist. Bill was also a good artist, but A. D. was a faster talker.

Bill and A. D. drifted into a little west Texas town about noon one day, and met a man with about as much grit as they had. He ran a café on Main Street. The screen door leaned ajar, but the smell coming from the kitchen was more than they could ignore. The café needed its window sign repainted. They had no money for lunch so they made an offer to repaint the sign for lunch and $10.00 cash. "I also need to have the ceiling of my café varnished, how much for that?" he asked.

"Another $10.00," Bill said.

"OK. You guys get started and I will fix your lunch."

Bill and A. D. finished their lunch and the sign. "We are finished, and we are ready for our money," Bill said.

"You haven't done the ceiling yet," he countered.

"No, we just want the $10.00 for the sign.

"You said you would do them both for $10.00." The owner stood about six foot tall and with his hand on a rolling pin. "You guys give me any trouble and I will call my friend, the Sheriff. Get the job finished or get out of town."

Bill started to argue, but A. D. called him off. "We will fix the ceiling," he said. "Let's get that half gallon of varnish from our truck, and we will get another half-gallon from the grocery store across the street", A. D. said.

"They don't carry varnish in a grocery store," Bill said.

"No, but they have plenty of Karo syrup I bet." They mixed the syrup with the varnish and painted the ceiling.

With their pockets lined with $10.00, the road out of town ran smooth and straight. They laughed and wished they could see the flies streaming through the front screen door to feast on the syrup painted ceiling. Some grit is rougher than others.

How to Spoil a Grandson

Somewhere in a cardboard box, hidden in a closet is a picture of me with my two grandfathers, and two great-grandfathers.

No, I have no idea where to look, but if I run across it, I am going to nail it to the wall over my writing desk.

The one I remember the most was my mother's father, William McCoy. I called him Grandpa. Grandpa was a successful farmer and rancher on the upper reaches of the San Gabriel Creek. I was his first grandson. And at that time, it looked like I might be the only one. I was not spoiled...just well catered to. Grandpa always planted a watermelon patch just for me to enjoy. Well, he let others enjoy the melons also, but I got first choice. How nice.

One summer I remember he took me swimming in the creek that ran through his farm. He jacked up his car, removed a wheel, let the air out, popped the tire from the rim, and pulled the inner tube from the tire. He hand pumped the inner tube full of air. Then we went swimming. I had a great time. I had no idea he would have to remount the tire to the car. I guessed that was what Grandpas did.

Grandpa let me fish for perch in his stock watering troughs. He had gone to the trouble of seining the fish from the creek and putting then in the stock trough. And I caught plenty of them. He insisted I learn to clean them and take them to the kitchen for Grandma to cook for supper. She did. I guess you could say she had a hand in spoiling me also.

Once, when I awakened from a forced nap, Grandpa had made me a little sailboat. He had shaped the hull from an old board, drilled a hole where the mast needed to be and inserted a stick. Wow! What a work of art. All we needed now was a sail. Grandma looked about and found a white cardboard box that marshmallows had come in and offered it for a sail. It made a grand sail. I figured all sail boats smelled like marshmallows. We were off to the creek. Grandpa launched our ship and my imagination took over. I could see that sailing vessel loaded with fish, netted from the clear waters of the Mediterranean Sea coming into homeport. The docks were lined with townsfolk, eager to purchase tonight's dinner. Then my mind saw a pirate boat, loaded with stolen gold and captured slaves, looking for a hidden, safe harbor. The captain was standing by the wheel spewing foul words at the crew. Then I smelled the cardboard sail. It wasn't a fishing vessel nor a pirate ship...It was a cargo ship. A cargo ship from the Orient, her sails bellowing and flags fluttering; a shining sight to a little kid sitting on a creek bank with his Grandpa. Surely, she was loaded with silks, silver, and spices. She was plowing the creek waters on her way to Boston for sure.

You can see what a lovely time we had sailing that ship. Today, when I smell a marshmallow, I can see that magnificent sailboat my Grandpa fashioned for me.

News from the San Gabriel

This week I got another letter from my good cousin, Jim McCoy. He lives way up the San Gabriel on an old dirt farm. It is always good to hear from him, even when the news is somewhat sad.

Dear Cousin:

I have some sad news from up here on the San Gabriel Creek. Old man Caleb Barnes died. I don't know if you knew Caleb Barnes or not. He was from one of the old families up toward Lampasas. Caleb was a big man, about six feet tall and almost that broad. He was a good farmer, but worried about living a long full life. In fact, it became an obsession.

Caleb heard of a healer and soothsayer that lived in a cave high on Old Baldy Mountain. The mystic could see your past as well as your future. He was gifted, it was said, to healing maladies, and prescribing natural cures for most ailments. Caleb climbed Old Baldy and found the Holy man sitting cross-legged, at the mouth of his cave, contemplating the world. Caleb asked, "What must I do to live a long, full life?" The holy man said nothing. He drew lines in the sand that lined the floor of his cave. He arranged colored stones into circles, then into lines. "There are two things you must do to live the kind of life you asked about," he said. "You must consume a teaspoon of gunpowder every day for the rest of your life." The old man sat silently, unmoving. Finely Caleb could not stand it any longer. "But what is the second thing I must do?" "When you die, you must have your body cremated," he said.

Well, Caleb went back to his farm and plowed his rows deep and straight. He out-lived three wives and a dozen fine plow mules. The porch was always full of kids and all their children. And each morning, with his coffee, he had a teaspoon of gunpowder. Folks asked about that practice. "It doesn't have much of a taste, kind of gritty, but it sure gives a fellow the power to finish the day's work.

The legacy Caleb left makes us assume that he followed the advice and that it in fact worked. He died last week at the age of 107. His legacy consisted of 6 children, 19 grandchildren, 23 great-grandchildren, 3 great-great-grandchildren, plus a thirty-foot hole where the crematorium used to be.

Hope this finds you and Alice in good health. Write when you can.

Cousin Jim

Cousins by the Dozens

Do you have a favorite cousin? I have one of every kind they make. My dad was the youngest of 18 children. If you do the math, you will believe I have one, and sometimes two of every kind of cousin that is possible. And that does not include the cousins on my mother's side of the family. As you can guess, most of my cousins were older than me. However, there were plenty of second cousins to go around. Some of the older cousins were a little hard on our society. One cousin was a little loose with the truth. He harvested hogs, regardless of their brand, and sold them to some unsuspecting stranger. The State of Texas rather frowned on that kind of business dealings. He spent a few years in the State Pen down at Huntsville. One of my uncles, not a cousin, stole an airplane, one piece at a time from the Army Air Force. He was able to wiggle out of that charge. Some strong talents race through our blood. However some of the kinfolks were as good as some were questionable.

Uncle Sam, a farmer out in west Texas, was also a lay preacher. He was as honorable as the others were sorry. When he died, the whole county turned out to pay homage to him. We even had one cousin who became a general in the U. S. Army. Darrell sure looked good, standing in his jeep, with medals and stars shining in the sun, as he led his battalion through our home town.

Cousin R. G. Stanford, from down near Victoria, called today. We got to remembering the outstanding qualities of our family. Some drank a bit too much, while others just made the stuff to sell. We counted the schoolteachers that came from our bunch...eight or nine I think. Cousin Dale ran for Texas Governor once. We were all proud of him for coming in 18th in a herd of 29 or 30 candidates'. However most of our cousins were just ordinary good citizens and parents. And that is no small accomplishment.

I began telling R. G. what a good member of our clan he is. He denied the charge. I reminded him of his successes with his family and business. I pointed out to him all his real estate holdings. I reminded him of the respect the folks have of him. His fair business dealings with his customers were a hallmark of his integrity. He tried to argue with me, but I refused to relent. I capped it off with the statement, "The city even named the street where you live after you. I don't think any of the rest of us can say that."

He got quiet on the phone, and I thought he had hung up on me. What I was waiting for was for him to return the compliments. And he did just that. "Well," he said "You know you had the good fortune, and sense to marry Alice. If it were not for her strength of character, good business knowledge, and driving force, you would be living under a bridge somewhere."

Building My Home Town

Do you have a secret desire to build a monument? An idea to leave a legacy that will last for years? An idea that will not make you rich, or famous, but says, "Hah, I did it." Have you had a grand idea to make a mark in the sand that says to the world, "I was here?" I think most men do. However they have been too modest to speak about it. Or they have reached a time when common sense tells us, "this is not going to happen."

I have reached that time. But, I am not so modest that I will not tell you about it. What

I have kept secret all these years is the desire to build a town. Yes! A town with stores, services, housing, schools, churches, a library, parks, sport fields, and perhaps a signal light or two. A town where all the power lines, and phone lines, are buried underground; no vulgar overhead lines hanging from creosote posts. A town where the city ordinances are realistic, flexible, and fair. A town where the sign ordnances are modeled after those in Hawaii or England. My town will always elect politicians that listen to the public, and understand who works for whom. This may sound a bit Utopian, but it could happen.

What would it take to accomplish this dream? First, I suppose, I will need to own about 100, 000 acres, half way between two other towns. The land needs to be fertile, sloping gently to the south until it meets a river that runs clear year round. The acres need to be divided east and west by a county road, and divided north and south by a State highway. The cross roads will become the center of this town. We will widen the roads, design an English roundabout for driving ease, and supply room for a sculpture of the namesake of this town...Lincolnshire, or perhaps Raeganville. The Ladies Garden Club could keep seasonal flowers planted and watered there. Clustered about the crossroads, like frogs at a pond, we will build the business section. The streets will be wide, curbed with sidewalks, and plenty of parking. No Wal-Marts please.

The North East quarter of the town will be reserved for schools and homes. There the playgrounds are open year round, and the swimming pool is free to all. The children may walk to class without having to cross a busy highway.

The South East quarter of the land will be used for all the services needed for a growing, thriving little town. City offices are built here. Also in this area are the school bus barns. Street and utility services will reside in this area also.

The South West acres will be reserved for the industrial park needed to support a town. Perhaps a furniture manufacturing business could be built here. Computer and high tech offices for research and development could find a home in this area.

That leaves the North West quarter of my town to develop. Since this is a dream, a fantasy, a wishful contrivance, I think I may as well indulge in the thing all the way. The

North West quarter has been discovered to sit over one of Texas's biggest, newly discovered oil field. The black gold is there to be pumped and shipped. Hah! Don't you know all this fanciful dreaming will be easy to come to fruition? There is just one small item that becomes the fly in the ointment...I don't own the 100, 000 acres.

Wonderful Glory of Spring

 Sunday's one half inch of rain sure did feel good. It sounded good too; a flash of lighting, the rolling thunder and then the patter of rain on our tin roof was so encouraging. I don't think we have had such a pretty rain this year, nor perhaps last year either. It may be my imagination but I fancy the grass has already turned shades greener. I know when the sun comes out natures colors will be impressive. Driving home from church, Alice remarked, "I fancied I heard the fields of bluebonnets giving a sigh of relief."

Our mall is covered with a grand splash of blue, the best we have had in several years. It is a puzzle to me that we have such a grand display of these handsome flowers. The soil has been dry for the last few years, yet this year, even without moisture, the area is covered with bluebonnets. Do you suppose they know something we do not know?

I enjoy mowing grass. In just a few days, I will have the pleasure of mowing. However, with the pasture covered with bluebonnets, I will need to be careful of cutting the flowers. In fact, it will take until sometime in May for the seeds to mature before I can mow the entire acres. I am told that only 40% of this year's seeds will come up next year. The other 60% lay dormant until the following year to germinate. That is an awesome safety devise to insure the bluebonnets success over the years. I suspect many plants in nature use this genetic lifeline. I know many spring flowers come up in the fall and grow roots down to be ready for the spring flowering. Anomie, larkspur, and paintbrush are a few I have observed using this device. There are probably hundreds more.

I have not been out driving the country looking for the wild flowers. I bet out west toward Llano, Mason, and Burnet the views are breath-taking. Have you had the heady pleasure of smelling a field of bluebonnets? Find a large field of these flowers, on a calm day, and inhale the fragrance. You will find it overwhelming.

You are invited to drive out to our place and see our display of these flowers. Drive in, make the circle, and stop for a picture or two. Carefully position the children close to the bluebonnets for a picture you will treasure for years. If you have time, come to the house, and Alice will make us a cup of coffee. We will sit on the porch swing and count our blessings.

Landing Strip in the Mountains

Homer was the youngest of nine children. Newly married to Lola, he scratched out a living as a tenant farmer. His older brother, Luther, was child number seven of the family. Luther had managed to leave the mountains of Morgan Creek and land a job in a warehouse for the United States Army Air Force, Kelly Field, and San Antonio, Texas. This was the nineteen twenties and cash money was rare. Luther, compared to most folks, was a rich man. He was able to buy a new car every year. He did as he well pleased. It pleased him to be a single man in the Roaring Twenties. He bought the home place on Morgan Creek. He owned a home in San Antonio. He had it all. Then the world was plunged into the financial crash of 1929 and the devastating depression of the 30's. However, Luther led a charmed life; the crash did not affect his life, except to make him bolder.

As most young men, Luther wanted more. And money is the fastest way to get more money. Prohibition and manufacturing, storage, transportation and sale of alcoholic beverages brought out the worst in many men of those times. Luther decided to get into the lucrative trade of running alcohol from the mountains of western Burnet County to the thirsty streets of San Antonio. He decided an airplane was the best way to move the product. Luther managed to beg, borrow, and steal a double winged, open cockpit, Waco airplane. Now he faced the problem of where to land his plane in the mountains, canyons, and cedar covered acres of Morgan Creek.

Aha! Little brother, Homer, may just be the answer to the problem. Luther talked Homer into cutting the cedar, dragging the brush, and toting the rocks from a strip just big enough to land and take off in his new Waco airplane with a load of alcohol. Homer attacked the task with vigor. He had never seen as much cash money as he was promised to complete the project. With that money, he mused, he planned to buy Lola a new dress, curtains for the house, a pair of stripped overalls for himself and son, and the moon if he decided. Winter was approaching, and the days were growing incessantly shorter. His ax biting into the aromatic cedar filled the glade with a pleasant sound that echoed up and down the canyon walls. Dragging the rocks was just back breaking work. However, by the first of December 1933 the task was completed.

Luther flew the Waco in and proved the strip was perfect. Scrounging the alcohol for the first delivery proved to be more trouble than planned. However, by the fifth of December the first load was ready for its flight to San Antonio. Then word came to

Morgan Creek; Prohibition has been repealed! Luther's well-planned scheme for easy money came crashing down. The bootleg business was gone, along with the vision of easy money.

So were the hopes for Lola's new dress, curtains, stripped overalls, and perhaps the moon. Vanished like a puff of smoke. But the landing strip lasted for years.

Building Chicken Nest Boxes

John Steel left word at Winkley's Hardware for me to stop by his place...soon. No telling how long ago he left that message. I drove to his rocky farm, way out county road 200, high on a hill overlooking North San Gabriel river. I managed opening his wire gate without cussing too much. "I am going to help John build a proper wooden gate that swings on hinges one of these days," I said to myself.

As I drove up to his shotgun house that old, spotted dog greeted me with a half-hearted bark and a lazy growl, then disappeared under the front porch. John was not sitting in his rocking chair on the porch. That was strange. I hollered "Hey, John."

"Down here at the chicken pen," he yelled.

I walked down past the windmill, his garden, and near the barn where his chicken pen sits. It is fenced to keep the larger chicken hungry varmints out, with a covered shed at the north end that can be locked at night to protect the hens and one feather-legged rooster.

"What are you doing down here, John?" I asked. "I am trying to build a nest for these setting hens. I don't have enough boards, and I am sure glad to see you. You got any old boards around your place you could loan a fellow?" I knew he had seen my stack of plywood, and figured I would part with enough to build a couple of nests for his setting hens.

That rooster was having a fit with my arrival and had herded his flock down to the far end of the pen. What a curious bunch of chickens John keeps. He has black ones, black ones with speckled necks, one speckled all over, and a few buff colored ones. "I used to have one white chicken, but the others picked on her until they finally killed it."

"John, let's go to my place and I will see if we can find enough plywood to build your girls a nest." We climbed into my pickup, with the spotted dog sitting in the middle, all eager for a ride. He managed to slobber all over both John and me during our drive.

Back at the chicken pen we measured, and sawed the boards needed to build two boxes about 16 inches square....or almost square. He nailed the boards together with a lip across the bottom of the open side. Proud as punch, John set the new nest on the ground of the shed, and filled the floor of the boxes with new hay. We moved the already setting hens and their eggs from the laying boxes into their new home. I noticed each egg had been marked, in pencil, with an X. "Why have you marked those eggs, John" I asked.

"Well, you see, when the setting hens come off the nest to eat and drink, the other hens lay a new egg with the older ones. With the setting eggs marked, I know which ones to remove. When I was younger, my mother marked the setting eggs with "Mrs. Stewart's Bluing. You know you can't find that in the stores now days. Let's go set on the porch and have a cup of coffee," he said. I knew he was referring to breakfast coffee warmed over. That stuff is strong enough to walk. I declined the offer, and headed for my pickup. "Well you just wait. I'm going to get you a dozen eggs for you to take home. Nothing like country eggs, homemade biscuits, and thick sliced bacon for breakfast. I bet Alice will be able to swing that in the morning."

Some Stories are Full of Bull

Doug McWhorter was a crusty old rancher that ran a bunch of hungry looking cows on a few sections of land west of town. He looked like his cows. Lean, mean, and unkempt. His boots had seen better days, and his Levi jacket had lost all its' color, and gained a few rips. He stood about five foot six inches tall. With a few days growth of beard he looked like he had just had a fight with a wildcat. But he was not a man to be pushed around.

Doug decided it was time to upgrade his herd. He bought a wild-eyed young bull from a neighbor, and turned him into his pasture. It was not long before the new bull was missing.

Years ago, the railroad had run a line right through the middle of his ranch. Kind of upset Doug. That started a running battle with McWhorter and the railroad. He claimed the line didn't pay much attention to the up-keep of the fences on each side of their right of way. The railroad bought several cows after the engine butchered a few of them. Horns and hide was about all that was left from those encounters. That was one way to market his cattle, but a little messy. Besides, he knew each cow personally. He hated for them to go to such an ignoble end as that. He had been pushed as far as his patience would allow.

Doug McWhorter brought suit against the railroad for the loss of his new, expensive bull. The case came to court. The railroad sent a young, dandy-dressed lawyer from Austin in their defense. Doug showed up a bit early and they had a pre-trial talk at the local watering hole. The lawyer argued for Doug to settle out of court. They discussed the merits of their differences. Finally, Doug agreed to settle for about half what he was asking.

The fancy lawyer wrote out a check, and Doug signed off on the settlement. With a grin, he pocketed the check. The lawyer just had to gloat about his clever moves. "You know old man, you just got taken. I knew I didn't have much of a case, and could not have won. The engineer was asleep in the cab, and the fireman was in the caboose when we roared through your ranch. You have got a lot to learn about this court business."

"Well I guess you are right about that ", Doug replied." I was a bit worried about winning myself. You see, that darned bull came home this morning."

Sometimes You Need a Little

Help Getting into Heaven

On the west side of the square of my hometown there were a multitude of stores. One of our favorites was the Western Auto Store. Jordan Everett ran the store and stocked many auto needs. The things we liked most were the bicycles and stuff to make them look neat. He had reflectors for our mud flaps, fancy handlebar grips, and even horns and lights for our bikes. New tires and patching equipment attracted us kids like magnets. The smell of the store was great.

Next door was Fry's Drug Store. We didn't care about the medicines he stocked, but what we liked was the soda fountain. Five cents bought a big cone of ice cream. I liked strawberry best, Charles Crawford liked chocolate. Often Doc Bowen paid for our cones, and he liked vanilla. So on those occasions we had vanilla.

A place that was off limits to us kids was Sam Field's Pool Hall. The smells that poured from the door seemed to be a mixture of chalk dust and tobacco smoke. We were cautioned not to even look inside the windows. We looked. The room was dark, lit only by mysterious green lamps. We heard strange clicking sounds, and raucous laughter from the inside. There were men standing around tables with sticks, poking little colored balls. Often the balls disappeared. That mystery was not solved for many years.

Two doors down was the Sawyer and Zimmerman Feed Store. They stocked most of the needs of the farmer and rancher. They had a running battle with Sam Fields. Both claimed ownership of a four foot, wooden stool. It was not a fancy stool. It had been repaired often, and showed plenty of ware. When one owner was out of the store, the other one stole the stool. Then that owner watched for a chance to steal it back. That went on for years, and their loud arguments were mostly bluster. I think both enjoyed the game. Years passed, and both stores closed. I never learned who ended up with the stool.

Butch Riggs Barber Shop fit between the two fighting stores. He didn't seem to mind. He was a Spanish American War veteran, and probably figured their differences fun to watch. What we liked about Butch's shop was the bright red and green bottles of tonic Mr. Riggs applied liberally to our fresh cut hair. We sure smelled better than Sam Field's Pool Hall.

Past the feed store was Gerald Lyda's Boot and Saddle Shop. New leather just attracts little boys. He gave us scraps of the new leather that we enjoyed. His art with boots and saddles soon waned. He moved to San Antonio and built the Towers of America. Some art, that.

Around there somewhere was Northington's Funeral Home. When a member of our community died, Mr. Northington placed his casket near the front window. Town folks could stop by and pay their respects to the departed. The family and friends brought flowers and placed them around the casket. Auk Chesnutt was an old bachelor that lived on his ranch way out past North Morgan Creek. He had some different ways that made folks notice. He always wore a pistol on his hip, even when he came to town. The law frowned on that style of dress, but Sheriff Riddell managed to look the other way. Eventually, Auk died. Mr. Northington fixed him up in a nice coffin and placed him at the front window. Mrs. Fry and her daughter, Peggy, walked home from Wednesday's church service, right by Northington's window. There lay Auk Chesnutt without a single flower on his casket. Mrs. Fry worried about that through the night. Next morning she cut two arms full of flowers from her garden and sent Peggy to the home with them. The folks there made two beautiful bouquets and placed one at the head of the casket, and the other at the foot. That eased Mrs. Fry's heart. I suspect that helped Auk to get into heaven.

Smells and Sounds of My Hometown

I was just thinking about the ease we have in using our tools, our equipment, and appliances today. Just push a button and the things work. Sawing a board, making coffee, or heating and cooling our houses just takes a flip of a switch. It hasn't always been that way. I was thinking of Mr. Greathouse's cotton gin in my hometown. As the summer's cotton crop began to be picked, Mr. Greathouse had to haul in a plentiful supply of oak wood to fire his steam boiler. The steam ran the machines that sucked the cotton from the wagons, ran the stands that separated the seed from the boles of cotton, and then ran the compresses that packed a wagonload of cotton into a compact bale of five to six hundred pounds. Mr. Greathouse started early those days to get a head of steam in his boilers to do the work. When the steam reached a certain pressure, the gin master sounded the steam whistle to alert the farmers he was ready to process their cotton. That mournful sound traveled round the countryside for miles. And the farmers came...by the dozens. Us kids found that an exciting time. That mournful whistle sound not only called the farmers, it called us kids. We jumped from bale to bale of cotton as it stacked up in the yard until Mr. Greathouse ran us away. To us that whistle was the sound of summer.

Bunk Gibbs ran a feed store at the northeast corner of the city's square. He stocked all of the needs of the valley's farmers. He had seed potatoes, tomato plants, farm animal's medicines, and a wide assortment of feed. He had feed for chickens, rabbits, hogs, sheep, and cattle. One item I liked that he stocked were the salt blocks. They came in white, yellow, and a rust red. I don't know what the difference was but they all tasted salty. Mr. Gibbs also ground the farmers seeds and hay into their own cattle feed. That was what I liked best. When a farmer asked Bunk to grind his feed into a mash, he didn't just flip a switch or push a button to start the grinder. Mr. Gibbs had to fill the gasoline tank of his one cylinder engine, check the grease in the gears, fill up the water tank, and prime the one spark plug with fuel. With his mighty arm, he then cranked the engine until it started. Sometimes that took a lot of cranking. However, when it started, the whole town knew it. With no muffler on the engine, it came to life with a bang. And it ran with an uneven series of bangs: BANG......BANG..BANG.........BANG. He soon had the entire area's folks attention: "Bunk is grinding feed again." That sound filled the town with explosions for the rest of the day. We liked that. I am not sure the rest of the town agreed.

On the north side of the square stood Mr. Norris's Shoe shop. The shop was built of board and batten with a wood shingle roof. It had a false front, an awning, and best of all, a board sidewalk. I often walked by just pretending it was still the "Old west," and hear my shoe heels on that walkway. The best part of the shop were the smells: New leather, flax sewing thread, and shoe polish. To repair a pair of shoes, Mr. Norris had many power tools. A power knife, for cutting the leather, a sewing machine, for attaching new soles, a grinder for smoothing the edges, and three horse hair buffer wheels to make the job look good. All of these tools were mounted, in a row, on his work bench. They were all powered by an engine out back of the shop. From that one power source a long flexible belt ran the length of the west wall to a pulley on a shaft, at the ceiling, that ran across the work space from wall to wall. At each tool, a belt, from the power shaft, came down to energize the tool. The belt controller handle hung down to about head high. When Mr. Norris was working a pair of shoes he looked like a symphony conductor at Carnegie Hall, arms reaching up for the shift leaver, his pacing left and right, and indeed, creating a work of art.

I think of these things now, each time I flip a switch or push a button. We have it kind of easy these days, don't we?

Rome Was Not Moved in a Day

A few years ago, a couple bought the vacant lot across the road from us. Pat and Larry McLaughlin proved to be great neighbors and friends. Larry said he was a homebuilder and proved it by building a beautiful home on that lot. Larry, Pat, Alice, and I spent many lovely evenings together. Then Larry sold the house, packed up and moved. I guess the wanderlust bug bit him. Each year they come through the area and we spend time together. I don't like the fact they moved, but I forgive them. They are young, healthy, and handsome, and they need to get that out of their system. That was about four years ago.

Before Larry left, he showed me a pile of building stones that was left from his building. He asked me if I would like to have them. I was in the act of building a small bridge across a dry gully and needed a few rocks to cover the approaches to the bridge. I said sure. Larry scooped up the stone with his Bobcat and dumped the load where I asked him to. I think I made a mistake. I pointed to a spot about 20 yards from my bridge. Right in the middle of a lovely area in the pasture. It was obvious someone was going to have to lug those stones to the bridge. And place them in an orderly manner. I asked Alice for help. She said, "Perhaps tomorrow." I hinted to several men I needed help and all agreed to come over some day and we would get the task done. "Someday" rarely comes around. At least this one hasn't. I hired two youngsters in the area to move the stones, and place them on the embankment. They worked most of the day, enjoying using the golf cart, to drag a few stones to the bridge. I guess they may have moved a dozen or so stones. They sure did enjoy driving the golf cart.

All of that happened three or four years ago. Each day, as I pass the pile of rocks, I say to myself, "Got to get those stones moved." I suppose there must be about three or four hundred building stones in the pile. Each summer the sunflowers grow strong in the pile. Johnson grass does well there also. For the last few years I mow as close to the pile as possible. But it still looks unsightly. I have thought about building a fence around the rock pile. Or perhaps park an old pickup truck in front of the rocks. Alice says," no way".

This year something strange happened. As I was going for the mail, I thought, "You know, there are only a couple or three hundred rocks that need moving. I can move three rocks a day, and in less than a year, I will have that pile moved. And I can mow the pasture unhampered. Alice will be proud of me. I will feel a sense of accomplishment. And the good Lord knows I need all three of those things."

I have never before made a New Year's Resolution. I have been blindsided. But it is done. I will move those stones if it sends me to the rest home. That, as I think of it, is not a bad idea.

Christmas in the Kitchen

I trust you had a lovely Merry Christmas. All the homes were strung with lights for the holiday. Each window glistened with trees all trimmed and shiny bright. Surely, Baby Jesus was honored across the land. Santa Clause had no trouble finding Johnny's chimney and left each stocking filled. I feared my stocking would be stuffed with lumps of coal. Surprise! My sock was filled. I got books, candies, a pocketknife, and bags of fancy coffee, a weather temperature gadget, and a Stetson hat. For an old man that is way more than I deserved. I kind of felt sorry for my old Stetson. It has plenty of sweat stains, cedar wax, and other marks of hard work. Now it hangs on the wall knowing it will not get to go to town again.

Each Christmas I have a bit of a problem. What gifts am I to get for the kids? We have found money always fits. I have discovered that cash beats gift cards. The cards are often lost or misplaced. Or the cards are not used to the fullest, leaving a few dollars not spent. Cash spends anywhere. But a Christmas gift for Alice?

I looked for jewelry as a Christmas gift for Alice. I did not find any she did not have. I looked for pretty blouses. I like white, frilly, high necked, long sleeved ones. Apparently they are not made anymore. I also like bright red blouses, however a quick glance in her closet there seemed to be a full stock of them. Alice has a full arsenal of mops, brushes, buckets, and cleaners. So those gifts are out. I don't understand the thing women call makeup. Even the sales lady could not help me. In fact Alice looks just fine to me just as she is. However, I needed a Christmas gift for Alice.

In my dilemma, sleep just would not come. I tossed and turned. I searched high and wide for an appropriate Christmas gift for Alice. I scoured the Christmas catalogs for ideas. I toured all the aisles of Wal-Mart, Lowes, and Winkle's Hardware, and found nothing fitting as a gift. Midnight snacks became a habit. I began to lose weight, and gain grouchiness.

Christmas Eve morning broke clear, warm, and dry. The birds sang overhead and the squirrels leapt through the trees. I felt rested. Euphoria enveloped me. I felt generosity flood my being. As clear as a bell the thought came..."Go to Sears." I went. Sure enough. There sat the perfect Christmas gift for Alice - a shiny white dish washing machine. She will be thrilled, I will be the hero of the year, and the dishes will be clean.

Old Chestnuts Still Bring a Smile

On the south side of the square of my hometown, at the far east end, was a somber, sophisticated bank. That bank just smelled like what we thought money must smell like. Mr. Galloway, the president, sat at a big desk close to the entrance. We figured he was always counting money or refusing loans. What impressed me was the outside east wall of the brick building. The complete wall, 40 or 50 feet long, was painted in Tuscan red with big bold letters in white, outlined and shaded in black that read "First State Bank." I figured that was what it meant: this is the very first. I thought that was neat. The very first State bank the world over. I was told that was not really so, but I didn't believe them; it was the first for me. In the years since the wall and sign have been painted over several times. I am pleased that in the last few years the painting has peeled away, revealing the old bold sign, "First State Bank." Drive by there some day and you can see for yourself. I still think it was the first.

Further down the square were Guthrie Howell Drugstore, Sidensticker's Men's Store, Dobb Warden's Barber Shop, then Lafarge Hardware. Mr. Lafarge's guns, nails, hammers, saws and all things for sale were displayed on shelves, all the way around the store with a counter keeping us from handling the merchandise. If you were interested in buying an item, he would get it from the shelf and let you examine it. Mr. Lafarge was a clever man with a penchant for creating neat things. He carved wooden chains from a solid block of wood with his super- sharp pocketknife. They were not for sale, just something he did to intrigue us kids. He also carved wooden cages with round wooden balls encased inside. I never understood how. He had an unusual habit as he swept the sidewalk in front of the store. When he saw you walking down the sidewalk, he waited until you were a step away, he then wheeled around and put the handle of the broom across the sidewalk about six inches high. He insisted you either jump or step over the broom handle. It didn't matter to him if you were a little kid or the Mayor. Jump or step over; there were no other options. I jumped.

All the way down the south side of the square, past Yarborough's Variety, W. H. Smith's Dry Goods, and Adam's Food store, then south down Main St about one half block was Hansford Stapp's Sheet Metal Shop. More importantly to us kids, out back was Dad Swift's blacksmith shed. And that was all it was, a shed. I don't think it could even keep the rain out. All day Dad Swift heated iron red hot, and hammered it into the desired shape. He was an artist with hammer and anvil. Farmers brought their plow points for him to sharpen with his muscled arms and steady beat. The music of his beating the metal on the steel anvil permeated the town square: a medley of lovely music.

Horse shoeing was his specialty. The steel shoes came in a standard shape and had to be heated red-hot, and hammered to fit the horse. For the rocky ranch land in those parts, it required each horseshoe to be shaped with a 'cork' at the open end to ensure the horse's footing. As each shoe was fitted, still red hot, it was tossed onto the dirt floor of the shed to cool.

One day Chum Wilson, intrigued by the blacksmith music, sauntered by. By now the horse shoes, still hot but steel color, lay in the dirt. Dad Smith bent down, picked up one of the shoes, yelled and flung the still hot shoe across the alley to Chum. Chum caught it and dropped it immediately. Dad Swift grinned and asked, "A little hot for you?"

"No" Chum said, "it just don't take me long to look at a horse shoe."

Father's Day Mystery

What do you know about your Grandfathers? Not much I would bet. One, my mother's father, had a mustache and Dad's father had a full beard. Somewhere I have a photograph of me sitting in the lap of one grandfather with the other grandfather and two great-grandfathers looking on. I could not tell if they were pleased or just sitting where they were told to sit. Not many of us are privileged to have that many grandfathers. The great-grandfathers probably came to Texas from Kentucky or Tennessee driving an ox-wagon loaded with the bare essentials of life and farming. The grand fathers were probably born here in Texas, I don't know. I don't really know much about my own father. He was always at home, ready to share a story or two, but I didn't ask. I didn't write anything down. Now I remember a few of his tales, but I fear they may have faded a bit in time.

Is there a box somewhere stuffed with papers of my great-grandfathers, chronicling their thoughts? Their hopes, their fears? Could those old men read or write? And why did they leave their kin and friends back in those eastern states to start anew? How did my grandfather's scratch out a living and save enough money to buy a farm or ranch? I know little about how hard my own father worked that allowed him to establish a store and handle the challenges of life. I never asked. I have now out-lived all my aunts, uncles, and cousins that may have been able to answer some of these questions. But I didn't ask. And there is my mystery.

However, there is an answer to this problem for you. It is easy to avoid this mystery in your life: just ask. Ask your folks about your grandfathers and grandmothers. Ask about your uncles and aunts what did they do, how did they manage such grand successes. Even write their mistakes or failures. Write their stories on a scrap of paper or on a tablet or in a journal. Stuff your box with their lives. In time, you can leave a store-house of memories for your children and friends, the story of their laughter, anguish, successes and failures. All will be a golden find for your children, even more for your grandchildren.

Today it is easy to avoid this mystery in your life. Bundle all your collected stories in an electronic file and send them to a self-publishing house. There are many in the business. I use Amazon. They will print you a proof copy to edit for less than $20.00. Edit your book, send it in with an order of a dozen or a hundred. In just a few weeks you will be a published author with lots of wonder and "atta boys".

Old Men, Little Children, and Watermelon Wine

Tom T. Hall wrote a song entitled something like that. I think he used the phrase, "Old Dogs," instead of Old Men. I figure old dogs and old men are about the same. They both lie around the house and don't do much. Maybe on warm days he will move out on the gallery, on the shady side, and take a snooze in a rocker. He also barks instructions to anybody that happens by. Scratch fleas? Sure he does, and swats flies too. He is just waiting for his "Missus" to call him to supper. He would really like her to bring supper to him on the porch, but he's too shy to ask. I think the little woman told him once, "Don't push it buster." That was good advice.

Speaking about age, ever notice how little children tell you how old they are? Say they are three or four they will add the months until they will be four or five. Now ain't that cute? That practice holds true through the teen years and sometimes even into the twenty's. But you let the years tumble into the thirty's and adding to their age stops...in its tracks. Say, about 39. That year sure gets used a lot. I remember getting to the 'magic 39' and I stayed there several years. Looking back I don't know why we do that. Fear of the future perhaps. Or the realization we have reached the half-way mark, and haven't accomplished much in our lives. That thought is an illusion.

We have family and they all think we are doing just fine. Buy a house about that time and the folks back home just know you wrote a check for the total price. "Paid for that house in full at the closing," they tell the folks around the square on Saturday mornings. Sure sounds good, but I have never known a young man who was able to do that. What we did was sign on for the rest of our lives to pay, each month, half of our pay checks. But during the forties, fifties, and sixties we accumulate a host of good friends. Shucks, they are all in the same boat, paddling like crazy, but having the time of their lives.

About then we reach the plateau of the 70's. The air is cool, retirement embraces us, and we began to understand many of the mysteries of life. Like grandchildren. That may be the best thing God ever invented. They are so cute and handsome, just like their Grandma and Grandpa. It makes you wonder why we didn't have grandchildren first, then our children. That is what makes the 70's so grand a time.

However, there is another mountain to climb...the eighties. The view from up here is breath taking. The world spreads out in what seems forever until it reaches the far horizon. The meadows are emerald green with silver rivers meandering through the land. The air is intoxicating, and moved by a gentle breeze. Blue skies every day...it only rains during the night, and gently at that. The snows that come in winter make the land into a fairyland. Of course the month of August is the best time of the year. That is the time when some of us count our years. And counting them to family and friends is what we do. We are prone to adding a few years if we are not careful. As Alice and I get older we're just like little children: we want to see next year, and grow up.

So there you have most of it, "Old Dogs, and little children..." I don't believe I have ever had a drink of watermelon wine.

The Culprit is Hiding in the Grass

A small shower of rain can turn a brown pasture of grass into an expanse of green. We have been favored with some rain lately. And that makes me happy. For you see, I like to mow grass. Sometimes I mow about five acres. I suppose being able to look back and see a lovely carpet of green gives me a feeling of having accomplished something. I find that while mowing I can put my mind in neutral and roam the world with my thoughts. Thoughts of faraway places around the world as well as those just down the street. Strange sounding names march through my mind, and I have no need to learn to spell them. While mowing I can fancy I feel the crisp mountain air blowing around my collar. Or feel the sands of the beach beneath my feet. That is about as magic as you can get.

And when I am finished mowing the pasture I find a shady spot, on a little rise, and survey my neatly trimmed domain. Often I dismount my metal steed and sit in the grass. On occasions, I lean back and watch the clouds drift by. It doesn't get any better than this.

It doesn't get much worse either. About midnight my lovely sleep was interrupted with an incessant itch. I itched behind my knees, around my waist, and all the tender spots on my body. Scratching just made it worse. Chiggers! Red Bugs! I went to my Funk and Wagnall reference books and looked up the culprit. *Trombiculidae* the big book informed me. That did not help. When dawn finely came, I hurried to M & L Pharmacy and pleaded for help. Larry suggested some fancy ointment. Carola helped me find the nostrum, and suggested I take a hot, soapy shower first. I wanted to tell her that it was not Saturday night, but thought better of it.

I went back to my big books and read further. *Trombiculidae*, chigger to you and me, is the nymph stage of an almost microscopic bug designed, I suppose, to keep us humble. It is worrisome but not dangerous. The little red-orange bug pierces our skin, injects saliva, and then sucks the juice into his body. He then falls away and completes his life cycle in the grass. That was more than I wanted to know.

Larry and Carola's suggestions were helpful...even though it wasn't Saturday night. Alice came to my rescue with a magic marker looking pen called "After Bite, the itch eraser." It did an admirable job of stopping the itch. Perhaps all three suggestions used together would be great.

I still enjoy mowing the grass. I have no intentions of quitting my sport. However, one thing is certain, I am not going to lie in the grass and contemplate the universe.

Letting the Wind Charge Your Batteries

When I was a young boy we took Sunday drives in the country, just for fun. Those dirt roads were narrow, crooked, dusty, and sometimes muddy, but they got you to the beautiful parts of the land. It was great fun, and it got Mom and Dad out of the house and barn for a few hours. Us children enjoyed it also.

We counted horses in the fields as a game. The person with the most 'counts,' won. Or sometimes we counted red barns, or black cows, or pigs in pens. Dad was best at the game. Sometimes he just pointed to let us little ones get a count. The winner of these games had the privilege of choosing what kind of treat we would have when the drive was over.

On these drives, I noticed, at many farms, a different looking thing to count. Sitting high on a tall post or stand was a motor looking thing, with a propeller at one end and a tail at the other. Dad called it a wind charger. So we counted wind chargers. However, I was curious, and wanted to know what the thing was. "Ask your Uncle Buck. He knows all about wind chargers," Dad said.

"A wind charger is an electric generating motor. The wind turns the propeller to let the motor create electricity. The tail keeps the motor pointing in the right direction. And all that keeps the radio batteries fully charged so we can hear "Lum and Abner" on Saturday nights, and your Aunt Drusilla can hear "Stella Dallas" each day," Uncle Buck said. "It is the newest thing."

I later learned that country folks in those days did not have electricity in their homes. To play the radio they had to buy batteries and keep them charged. It was expensive to take the batteries to town for re-charging. So the Zenith Radio Company built battery charging units to solve the problem. The Wincharger, as they called them, sold for $15.00, a pricey amount in those days. However, the radio was an important luxury each home wanted. They designed the Wincharger to meet the need.

I later learned Uncle Buck did not have $15.00 to buy one of Zenith's Wincharger units. However, Uncle Buck was an ingenious and clever man. He scrounged a generator from an old wrecked car. Buck then fashioned a tail from a piece of metal he removed from the barn. With a sharp drawknife, shingle hatchet, and saw he made a propeller from a length of two inch by six-inch pine board. Putting all this together, in just the correct way, he had his wind charger. Buck fastened all this to a tall post, and kept his radio batteries charged just fine with little cost.

At some abandoned farm home, down a dusty back road, you may see a Wincharger still standing. It might work. If you do, call me. I would like to see it. Or better yet, do you think you can build a Wincharger for your Ipad? I bet your Uncle Buck could.

Riding the Wind With a Thumb

and a Prayer

Eugene Pirtle and I arrived in Abilene, Texas about mid-morning. The sun shone brightly through the brisk November air. His destination was home to Burnet, mine was Bisbee, Arizona. He headed south and I turned west with a casual good bye.

We were not traveling on a bus, train, car or plane. We were traveling on a by-gone method of transportation that has gone with time. It lasted from the advent of the motor car and ended with the turbulence of the 1960's and 70's. We called it "Hitch Hiking," or "Thumbing." One could walk to the edge of town, face the on-coming traffic, stick up your right hand with thumb extended, and soon a passing car would stop and take you on down the road. It took patience, neat dress, and a pleasant smile but soon you had a cheap, comfortable ride. Sometimes soon was not the proper word.

Dark comes quickly in November. Standing on the western edge of Abilene the weather turned colder, and wet. Now where was I to spend the night? I thought about looking for an unlocked car to take shelter when a big, old Buick car stopped. A black man asked me if I could drive. "Sure," I said. Would I mind driving them, they were going home to Los Angeles and could not find a motel that would accept a black family. I got behind the wheel and happily drove out of Abilene westward at last.

The Stark family of daddy, mother, and two girls must have been driving a long time, coming from Mississippi that day at 45 miles an hour. Mr. Stark said his mechanic had warned him not to drive any faster for it could cause car trouble. That is not what a young boy with a heavy foot needs to hear.

However, I managed, with Mr. Stark's eye constantly on my driving speed. We crawled through Sweetwater, Midland, Odessa, and Monahan with only a view of the road and oil field burning flairs. By the time we got to Pecos I was bushed. It must have been two or three in the morning I found an all-night café open. I stopped for a Coke Cola. A big, unsmiling Sherriff, packing the biggest chrome plated, pearl handled six-shooter I have ever seen walked up to my stool. "You with those black folks in that Buick out there?" He asked.

I said, real quickly and politely, "Yes sir."

"Well, it is about time you got them out of town. I did just that.

We parted ways in El Paso about daylight and I thumbed a ride with Mr. and Mrs. Art Thompson. They were just retired from the railroad in Michigan and driving to see the Wild West. There is no telling what stories I told them. I stayed as close to the truth as I could with as much color as I dared. What a pleasant day we had.

The next morning the Thompsons turned north at Lordsburg, New Mexico and I, at the edge of the town "thumbing" west to

Douglas, Arizona. Bill Bryson, a shoe salesman from Chicago driving a brand new Chevrolet picked me up. About halfway to Douglas he ran out of gasoline. The west is big on open spaces and vacant stretches of roads. That Easterner had no way of knowing what to do. I became his hero. I suggested I hitch hike to the nearest gas station, get a can of fuel, and bring it back. He gave me five dollars, I "hitched" a car, and left him stranded in the absolute middle of nowhere. I wondered what he thought. I awakened a gas station attendant, bought three gallons of gasoline, paid a five-dollar deposit on the can and "hitched" a ride back to Bill's stranded, brand new Chevy. He bought my breakfast in Douglas.

I was soon in Bisbee, AZ. My Aunt Pearl and Uncle Bill welcomed me to their state. For the next month, I was shown all around a new world. Copper mines, hunting camps, and the best food west of home was the order of the day. The days fled quickly and it was time for me and my trusty thumb to go home.

The adventure of hitch hiking a thousand plus miles was a grand experience for a young boy with little knowledge of human life. However, times have changed. I would not advise trying it in today's times. Sad. We just lost a bit of Americana.

Snoring

Sometime in the middle of the night, Alice gave me a rude shake. "Turn over. You are snoring. I can't get any sleep with that noise." Guess you know what I did. I turned over quick. Lying there, I was amazed. I did not know I snored. I thought just older men snored in their sleep. Then I remembered one of our uncles. Uncle Newt was in his wandering years, and had no home of his own. He traveled from one of his kin folks to another, and stayed with them until they politely suggested perhaps he should move on. It didn't seem to bother Uncle Newt, so he moved on. Uncle Newt stood perhaps five foot or so tall, but may have been the hill country's best cedar chopper. That is how he managed to support himself and his way of life, which was working, drinking, and fighting. It seemed to work well for him.

Those activities perhaps caused one of his bad habits...snoring.

I remember when it became our lot to house Uncle Newt. He moved in with only one pair of work pants and shirt, and one dress shirt and pants. Those few clothes, a chopping ax, and an old car he had cut down and made into a work truck was all he owned. However, he worked hard all week in the cedar brake and managed to fill his truck by Friday with cedar posts. Saturday morning early, he sold his week's work, came to our house, took a bath, shaved, and left for a day and night of drinking and fighting.

Dad admired Uncle Newt's hard work, tolerated his drinking, and prayed for his safety in fighting. He had one habit that he could not be excused for...snoring. Each night Uncle Newt fell into bed, exhausted from work, fell asleep and snored all night long. The buzz saw sound permeated the house from rafter to floor, and through walls. Then the sound would stop. Then start with a cough, a sputter, and again the buzz saw. None of the family got much sleep. Dad suggested Newt sleep on his side. No help. He still snored. Dad suggested he sleep on his stomach. Did not help. Still that raucous sound rattled the house. I guessed it was shaking the windows. No, I am sure that was what was happening.

Dad thought of asking Uncle Newt to sleep in the barn. However, there was no water in the barn. No lights either. No bath. No heat. Only one option was left for Dad. He asked his brother to find another kin folk to keep awake. With a laugh and smile, Uncle Newt took his meager processions and left in good humor.

I now have come to the understanding I might have reached the age of mankind to start snoring. I don't think Alice wants me to pack my things and find other folks to keep awake. I do a fair job of bringing her morning coffee to her bed each day and I cook a mean breakfast. And she likes the way I keep the yard mowed. We do have a well house with lights and water. I have given that some thought. But winter is coming and there is no heat out there.

I am working on a solution to my snoring. Perhaps some of you folks might have a suggestion. In my desperation, I will entertain them all.

Two-year-old Black Colt

My Grandpa Baker had 18 children. I am not sure he knew all of their names. His first wife gave him seven girls and two boys. His second wife produced seven boys and two girls. My Dad was born in 1905 and was the youngest of the 18. The oldest of the first batch of kids he named Basil. Grandpa Baker moved from La Grange, Texas to Burnet County out on Morgan Creek in 1884. Uncle Basil followed soon after. Uncle Basil had saved enough money to buy a farm just west of the town of Burnet. He raised all the needs of a growing family, like tomatoes, potatoes, and a lot of Glimp beans. He produced those farm products he could sell for a handsome profit. The lower field, being a sandy patch of ground, was just great for peanuts and watermelons. Both were popular with the town folks.

Uncle Basil found another product that was needed by the folks in town...firewood. During the week when the farm did not demand his attention, he cut live oak logs.

He loaded them in his wagon, hitched his mules, and drove the two miles to town early Saturday mornings. He tied the wagonload of stove wood in the shade of a giant Live Oak tree just behind Bunk Gibbs Feed Store. For the rest of the day Uncle Basil walked around the town square visiting folks that had come Saturday shopping. Noontime he made his way down to Maudie's Café and had a bowl of chili. Cost him five cents. A bucket of oats and five gallons of water for his team was free. Basil never tried to sell his wood. Everyone knew he brought stove wood to town on Saturdays. If you needed wood you had to find him somewhere on the square and make a deal with him. Some weeks he did not sell his wood. Didn't seem to bother Basil. He just untied his mules and made his way home, taking that load of wood with him. He figured there was another Saturday coming in about a week.

Horse-trading was not only a sport, but also a need. One fall day a fast talking horse trader drifted through the country with the most beautiful black, two-year-old filly Uncle Basil had ever seen. The horse stood about seven hands high and was broke to ride. He bought him. Basil made up some excuse to ride that beautiful horse to town that next day. He saddled "Beauty" with his best gear, donned his big black Stetson hat, dress jacket, and went to town...riding high in the saddle. About the first feller he saw on the town square was Jess Thomson. Jess was shocked. He said he had just bought that horse from a horse trader two days ago. Fact was Jess Thomson was a lot more than shocked, he was mad. Jess accused Basil of stealing his horse. Jess turned on his heel and headed to the Sherriff Chris Dorbandt's office to file a complaint. Basil followed. Sherriff Dorbandt was friends with both men and talked them into an unusual trial by fire, so to speak. The Sherriff got them to agree to meet at three o: clock that evening and see which man the horse would come too when called. In the meantime, Sherriff Dorbandt said he would track down the horse trader that had sold them both the same horse. They agreed. That afternoon, at three they all met at the square. Jess Thomson and Uncle Basel stood a few yards apart on the open square. The black filly was turned loose about 20 yards away from the men. The Sherriff's idea was which one the horse went to was the rightful owner. "Beauty" came straight to Uncle Basil. He mounted his horse, turned, doffed his black hat, and road out of town.

What Basil did not tell anyone until years later was, waiting for 3 o'clock that afternoon he had gone by Bunk Gibbs Feed store and gotten both pockets of his jacket filled with oats.

Sundays at Wingren's Stock Tank

Sunday morning was an ordeal for us boys. Dad insisted we get ready for Church early. The first thing we were to do was to polish our shoes with that black stuff that got all over our hands. That took another washing to remove the unwanted polish. We then donned our cleanest white shirt and a choking necktie. On us littler boys, the tie hung down to our knees. Mom usually had a clean and ironed pair of khaki pants for us to wear. We had to wear a dress jacket that was usually a hand-me-down of some unknown color. Dad inspected our fingernails and insisted we clean them with our pocketknives. We then had to sit quietly and wait for the rest of the family to get ready to walk the few blocks to church.

Mom checked on our dinner cooking in the oven and we were off to hear a long sermon. We went early and stayed late...but finally the walk home was great.

Dad insisted we wear our Sunday best at Sunday dinner. We managed. After dinner Dad gave the evening prayer that rambled on from the weather to our health of nation, state, and family. He then released us from our imprisonment and we were free for the afternoon...after we hung our Sunday clothes on coat hangers and placed them in the closet.

If it were summer time, the agenda's top item was a swim in Old Man Wingren's stock tank. We raced up the creek to where the tank awaited our arrival. As we approached the down side of the earthen dam, we began peeling off all our clothes. All trying to be the first to leap into the water with laughter and a shout of abandoned joy.

Up the stream about a mile, where the dirt road crossed the creek on a rattletrap wooden bridge, stood Ebenezer Primitive Baptist Church. Pastor Tommy B. Rivers held church most every Sunday until someone was encouraged to come forward, kneel at the altar, and confess. A confession was a sure ticket to the baptismal pool...Old Man Wingren's stock tank. That Sunday Sister Mary Jane's big sister Ellie finally promised to give up her wild ways and give her life to Christ. Shouts of joy and plenty of Amens filled the little church to the rafters. The march down the creek to the stock tank was a joyous trek. Pastor Rivers, with the help of Deacon Brown, led the large sister, Ellie, into the waters waist deep at the upper end of the pond. As Pastor Rivers held Ellie, leaning back a bit with his hand raised to give the prayer of successful conversion of a sinner, us boys reached the top of the pond's dam, spat naked, and jumped into the water with a shout. Ellie spotted us boys in natures undress and with a jerk yelled, GOOD GOD ALMIGHTY! She slipped from Pastor's grip and disappeared beneath the water. Deacon Brown helped the Pastor to bring Ellie up just as us boys realized we had interfered with God's handywork and beat a hasty retreat. Upon seeing our hasty retreat, Ellie gave the watching congregation another expletive and sank below the water again.

We never heard from Pastor Rivers about the rude interruption of the two baptisms Ellie got that Sunday. You can be sure we never told Dad about the adventure. I hope you will not tell about it either.

Pecan Harvest is Upon Us

Thomas Jefferson planted and nurtured pecan trees on his Monticello farm. Always a man in search of new and productive plants he nurtured the new world tree. He found the tree hardy, productive, and delicious. He shared his trees with President George Washington, who was an avid planter and gardener at his Mount Vernon home. A few years ago, I took a page from their book and planted a pecan tree in our back yard.

Through the years new varieties were developed. Today we have several choices of trees to plant. Different varieties do well in the different soils we have here in central Texas. The Caddo, Pawnee, Choctaw trees are popular, as are Stewart and Desirable. I suspect some of the names came from the fact that the Indians enjoyed the nuts of the trees, and shared their knowledge with the early white man that came to the new world. Some folks go so far as to say, "If it has an Indian name, it is good." Darwin Wiggers has a beautiful pecan orchard, and planted several different cultivars. I haven't asked him which tree he likes best. With his carefully kept records of his tree's production, I bet he knows. I have no idea what kind of pecan tree I planted. The nurseryman said, "This is a good tree to plant." That statement would just about cover any tree. Especially if you are selling trees. I do remember it cost about $50.00.

Down in our meadow, near the creek, we have several native pecan trees. Over the years, the drought has taken many of the younger trees. However, the older ones, with deeper roots, have survived. The largest one is for sure a native tree. Most years it has a few pecans, some years more. But never, in my observations, a bumper crop. They are small: about a half inch long, with a hard shell protecting the meat. However, the squirrels, crows, and blue jays have little trouble stripping the tree.

I dug a hole, deep and wide, and brought good dirt to cover the roots. I piped water to my prized pecan tree. It grew well. Three years ago, it bloomed. I was excited. It was loaded with about two dozen pecans that seemed to grow over night. Daily I inspected my tree. The husk split, and I decided to pick one tomorrow to taste. Too late. The squirrels beat me to every nut on the tree. Next year the tree put on several nuts. I covered the tree with a net to keep the rascals from beating me to the harvest. They came up the trunk, under the netting and again got all the pecans. This year I was determined to beat them to the draw. I installed steel posts around the perimeter of the tree and laced it with an electric wire. Hah! That did the trick. The grass grew tall and shorted the fence. I unplugged the electricity, and trimmed the grass from around the tree. The pecans had split their husk and tomorrow I could get my first harvest. Too late. In my smug, arrogant manner, I had forgotten to re-plug the electricity to the fence. They stripped the tree. Foiled again.

Next year I am going to build a wire netting fence all the way around my pecan tree. I will also have a top on the structure. I intend to install the thing with an electric wire. Perhaps I can get Alice to remind me, each day, to check the fence. I may buy Alice a new shotgun and ask her to stand guard. That will fix their bandwagon. Then when I harvest my pecans, I can decide what tree I planted.

It Could Be a Long Dry Spell, But I Doubt It

I bet I can tell what you are thinking. You think I can't read your mind? Watch this, then tell me I can't know what you are thinking. You are thinking, "Is it ever going to rain again?" Am I right? I thought I would be. When I was a kid, during a prolonged dry spell, I asked my Dad "Is it ever going to rain again?" His reply was, "There has been only one time in history when it didn't rain." I jumped at that, "When was that Dad?" "This time," he said. Well, you know that didn't last long. It rained. Now this time could be different, but I doubt it.

We all spend a lot of time worrying about the lack of rain...or too much rain. Now I agree both cases can be a problem.

However, our worrying about it has little effect on the situation. Remember the old movies about rainmakers. They showed up in the dry times and ballyhooed the folks into thinking they could make it rain. They collected the dry farmers hard-earned money, squirted chemicals into the air, shot off dynamite from a far hill, and filled the air with smoke. At the town square, he promised rain in the next three days and took up another "love offering." In the next three days, he was far away in the next county never to be seen again.

Our language is full of sayings about the weather. Some may be true: some may be wishful thinking. Here is one I haven't heard in years, "The talk of weather is nothing but folly: when it rains on the hill it suns in the valley." I can embrace that saying...most of the time. I have seen it just the opposite.

One saying I have noticed is usually true. "Rain before seven, quit before eleven." I cannot imagine why, but it often happens that way. Sam Weston, who used to hide out at the feed store said, "You better be glad it rained at all." He liked those days. He could not work in the rain, and when it stopped, the day was about gone. "Shucks,

I believe I will just go home and take a nap," he would say.

"Rainbow at night, sailor's delight, rainbow in the morning, sailors take warning." I like that saying. I bet it most often happens that way. In fact, I have seen only one rainbow in the morning. It sure was pretty, but I can't remember if I took warning or not. Of course, I am no sailor.

One thing I remember was the ring around the moon. Here in the country we keep an eye on the moon's comings and goings. I can't remember the last time I saw a ring around the moon. Some of the rings were big, and some were snug, up close to the moon. I am not sure what all that means. Some wag said there was a layer of ice crystals way high in the air, and the moon shining through it caused the ring to form. Perhaps that is a precursor of coming weather. No rings, no weather? It is possible. Grandpa said you could count the stars inside the ring and know how many days away the coming weather was. I never tried counting the stars and then counting the days until the weather changed. The next time I see a ring around the moon, I am going to keep score and see if all this is true. If you get a rain anytime soon, send some of it our way. It sure is dry here on the Shin Oak Ridge.

Life on the Farm

Dad's farm was not the richest one in the county, but it was not the poorest one either. Dad planted oats and wheat in the late fall. They came up and supplied grazing for the livestock through the winter. Springtime brought on a growth that matured with heavy heads of grain. The harvest supplied feed for the horses and flour for our table. The same fields were then planted in corn for fattening hogs and making corn meal and hominy for our summer dinners. The corn harvest was important feed for all the farm animals: chickens, hogs, and horses. The horses were needed to pull the plows and wagons that gave some mobility for the farm. A trip to town in a horse-pulled wagon took about three hours as well as three hours back home. The trips to town were needed to supply those items not raised on the farm:

baking powder, yeast, salt, sugar, sewing supplies, and most important, tobacco for Dad's pipe.

One of most important crops Dad planted was cotton. The cotton crop was one of the few farm products that supplied a cash income. Cotton needs some early rains to produce a sturdy plant. The plant then can produce an abundance of flowers. It is a grand sight to see a field of cotton in full bloom. The blooms soon become cotton bolls. The bolls are about the size of a hen egg and are great to throw at your brother. However, you had better be ready to run after you bounce a thrown cotton boll off Johnny's ear. Now you understand I never did that, but I have heard of mean old boys doing such deeds.

August's dry heat is just great for the cotton crop. Inside the cotton bolls, something magic happens: a fluffy handful of soft fiber develops. The boll soon matures and pops open to reveal a white fluff of rich fiber. Now the work begins. All the family is required to be in the fields for the harvest. Each person drags a sack with a strap that fits around the shoulder to hold the picked cotton. Dad's wagon sits at the edge of the field, waiting to be filled with the white cotton.

The wagon also has a jug of water and today's dinner. Mom made the lunches early in the morning with biscuits, bacon, and fried potatoes. Wow, that tasted good. The shade under the wagon was welcomed also.

I never picked much cotton. For two reasons. It was hard work, and the pay was not much. I did like riding on Dad's cotton sack, and playing in the creek down by the parked wagon. Often Mom included with the lunches a biscuit filled with molasses. A few crumbs from the biscuits thrown into the creek attracted plenty of fish. Now that interested me; catching fish. I never caught one, but the idea was always there. After much work in the field, the wagon was filled with cotton. Dad drove the horse-drawn wagon to the nearest cotton gin and had the crop processed. A wagonload usually made a 400 to 500 pound bale of ginned fiber. Late on ginning day, Dad came home with a check for the cotton and a pretty dress for Mom. Of course, us kids got a toy, and often stripped peppermint candy. I was always glad when the last of the cotton was picked and processed. Then I could get back to climbing trees and sliding down the cellar door.

FLOSSEY Bakes a Great Loaf of Bread

Alice's brother Eugene and I went all over Wise and Clay county Texas seeing the sights of that part of North Texas. I didn't see Alice. Well, I guess I did see her all dressed out in a Sears & Roebuck dress, and sporting a pair of pigtail braids that reached to her waist. Some little sister. However, a 19-year-old man doesn't pay much attention to pigtailed little girls.

However, I sure did pay a lot of attention to Alice's mother, Jessie. She knew how to cook for two hungry boys. In fact, I fear we ate most all she had in her pantry. The morning we left Jessie's home, we got out of bed early to the best smelling breakfast one could imagine. She had gotten up extremely early and killed a chicken, dressed it, and had it frying in a skillet. While that was cooking, she made a big-boy-bowl of flour gravy. But what got my taste buds bubbling was the bread from the oven. Mrs. Jessie said, "And for your two young men, my special FLOSSEY bread." She set three of the most beautiful golden, steaming hot, loves of yeast bread I had ever seen on the table. She sliced a loaf of that grand bread, passed it around, followed by home churned butter, and we were off to the best breakfast this boy had tasted. The gravy and fried chicken was good, but served with FLOSSEY bread it would make New York's best chef jealous.

With a lot of trials and tribulations, I finally grew up. The next time I saw Alice she had really grown up. Gone were the pigtails: her coal black hair coiffured and an uptown dress made a man take a second look. The following years were like a walk in the woods. I asked Alice two questions; would she marry me, and could she make FLOSSEY bread. She said yes to both questions.

I must admit, I forgot all about the FLOSSEY bread with all the work, family, and other things a young couple have to attend too. Not long ago I asked Alice if she knew how to make FLOSSEY bread. "Sure," she said. "All those rolls you have been eating were made by Mothers FLOSSEY recipe." I asked, "Why did she call it FLOSSEY bread?" Alice explained,

"Each letter stands for an ingredient in making the bread."

> **F** is for six or seven cups of flour.
> **L** two cups of warm liquid; water or milk.
> **O** one fourth cup oil.
> **S** one table spoon salt.
> **S** one third cup sugar.
> **E** one egg.
> **Y** three envelopes of yeast.

"Mix all this together, let it rise for an hour, work it down, place into three loaf pans, let it rise again, then bake until golden brown," Alice said. I tried it, and to my surprise, it worked great. Beginners luck? Nope, it works every time I have tried the recipe. And you know I am a little clumsy in the kitchen.

Just look at the bargain I got from Mrs. Jessie; A beautiful lady, and a great loaf of bread.

Deer Hunting Way Up Morgan Creek

"Hey, Hollis, get a bed roll together. We're going deer hunting," Dad said. It was late November and the nights were colder than kraut, but the days were warm. I was excited to be going on an outing with my Dad. I grabbed a couple of quilts, my hat from the rack at the door, and my new Winchester 30-30 rifle. Dad loaded the pickup with all the stuff we needed, and we were on the road.

"Where are we gonna hunt, Dad," "I asked.

"Way up Morgan creek. We will stay in an old camp cabin, if it is still standing," he said. The road to the cabin got rougher and rougher as we climbed the mountains and plunged into the next ravine. We soon came to where the years of rain had washed the road away and there was no driving any further.

"We will have to pack everything in from here," Dad said. That quickly became a task. Dad stopped, took his ax and went into the woods. He soon returned with a forked, flexible, cedar stick about six feet long. He laced the fork with rope, and then piled all our gear on a net he had brought. We each had a short rope we hitched ourselves to and dragged the travois looking thing the rest of the way to the cabin. We were exhausted but pleased the cabin was still intact. It had a wood burning stove for heat and cooking. The entire cabin was covered with dust and cobwebs that had collected over the years. We quickly cleaned a bit, and Dad started supper. Salmon patties and hominy tasted good after a day of getting to the cabin.

The cold night sounds were intriguing to a town boy. The creek gurgled pleasantly as a low elm limb scratched the roof menacingly. The noises soon became soft music filtering through the cabin walls, which quickly lulled me to sleep.

In what seemed to me the middle of the night, Dad ordered, "Come on son, we need to be at the clearing before daylight." It was easy to see there was not going to be any breakfast, so I grabbed the last of the salmon patties and stuffed it into my jacket pocket. Cold salmon patty for breakfast? Beats nothing. A gibbon's moon lit the way to our hunting ground. The moon light cast long shadows of strange shapes as we made our way. We settled ourselves with our backs leaning against an oak tree with a good view of the clearing.

The darkness was strangely quiet. No stirring of birds, rabbits, or any living thing. The warmth of my jacket and Dad's close body lulled me to sleep. The next thing I knew was Dad's gentle nudge..."Wake up son, your snoring will scare the deer away." I marveled at the beauty of the sunrise. The sky had turned from an inky black to a soft pink with a few streaks of clouds drifting north. The clouds and sky soon became a brilliant orange and the sun quietly came up.

And there we sat. And sat. Nothing stirred except the birds, rabbits, and a fox or two. No deer. Setting became a chore, but we dared not move much. Then breakfast. Cold fish never tasted so good. Dad said he wasn't hungry, and I was kind of glad. I ate it all and licked my fingers. About nine o'clock dad nudged me and I saw a lone deer at the end of the clearing. I counted its horns. Eight? No, ten. We had been working towards this moment. Dad said, "You take him." I raised my rifle, placed my front bead sight on his shoulder, then the notched sight just so. "Squeeze the trigger," said dad. I looked down the barrel. There only 40 yards away stood our trophy. I looked again. Bambi. NO! Not Bambi. I could not pull the trigger. Dad's gun downed the deer with a well-placed shot. Bambi fell just a few yards from where he was shot. Seeing the deer lying there, I realized this is what we came for. It was not Bambi at all. Just another wild deer.

Dad dressed the deer and we carried him back to the cabin. Fried back strap with spoon biscuits and gravy never tasted so good.

Now the deer's head is mounted and hangs on the wall near our front door. It holds my "gimmy" caps as well as my Sunday felt Stetson. Dad had a brass plaque inscribed, "Bambi" and attached it to the mounted deer's board. I do not intend to go deer hunting again.

A Battle at New Brinsley West

We call our few acres "New Brinsley West" in honor of our friends that live in New Brinsley, England; a lovely village in the Robin Hood Country. They know how to grow beautiful flowers. I am now engaged in a battle to the bitter end over a patch of Zinnias.

Many years ago, I spaded up a flowerbed at the entrance to our place. I made a mental note to ask our son, Greg, to plow the bed next year. I planted Zinnias and over the years, they have bloomed magnificently. The neighbors seem to enjoy them, and Alice likes to keep an arrangement on the dining room table. The butterflies enjoy the blossoms adding to the beauty of the flowers. Even humming birds find a sip of nectar at each blossom. I was surprised to find the night critters and bugs ignored our flowers.

Then came the years of drought. One year I spent over $300 on water for that little patch of beauty. I felt sure it would rain next year, but alas, no rain. I gave up the chase. The next few years I mowed the weeds where the flowerbed used to be. It has been sad, coming home with no splash of color to welcome us at the gate.

This year I decided we needed the flowers. Greg plowed the bed and I planted the Zinnias. They came up with a glory for life. Each morning I check their progress, water if needed, and weed the bed. I carry my tools, water hose, and myself to the road in an old electric golf cart. I got out and in my careless manner, I tossed a shovel into the cart, and turned to my task. The shovel landed on the go pedal of the cart, and it drove right across the flowerbed and into the pasture. I chased it down and drove it back to the flowerbed. I was able to save most of the young plants. A few dogs have found the bed is a handy short cut to home. It is amazing how often they can step square in the middle of a young plant. But I like dogs and I forgive them their trespasses. However, I am not sure I can forgive the new villain in the neighborhood.

White tailed deer. A doe and her fawn have a sister with twin fawns that live in the woods. They have discovered Zinnias taste good. The first morning I noticed their night raid they had nipped the buds from a half dozen plants. Maybe they just made a mistake in sampling the now 10 inch tall plant. Next morning they sampled a dozen or so flowers. Something had to be done to keep the bed from becoming a total disaster. I set post, and strung an electric wire around the bed. They just happily jumped the wires. I thought about buying some cattle panels from Winkley's Hardware. Then my anger subsided and I realized a fence would hide the beauty of the flowers. Deer repellant! That just may be the answer. I found a recipe in my set of Funk and Wagnall Know-it- all books that was guaranteed to keep the errant animals away. Eggs; old ones preferably, peppers; all colors; buttermilk; soured, and anything that stinks. Alice suggested a pair of my socks. Good idea. So I mixed all that up and set in the sun to ferment. Hooboy, it sure does that. Last night I gave the plants a good sprinkling of the concoction. This morning I hurried to the road for an inspection. No new plants were eaten.

If this smelly stuff works, you come by in a few weeks and we will cut you a bouquet of stinking grand Zinnias.

When *Scorpio* Rules the Night Sky

Summer days on the farm were grueling. The work was hard, and hot. The rows of cotton and corn stretched out in front of us with no end in sight. When Dad got ahead of us, the older boys would chunk a boll of cotton or ear of corn at us younger kids. We yelled "Dad, make Otis quit hitting us." Of course, Otis feigned innocence, but I think Dad knew what was going on behind his back. About the middle of the afternoon, when the sun burned down our necks, Dad would say, "Lets finish this row and the next one and we will rest in the shade." What a wonderful sound that made to our youthful ears. "Otis, you go to the spring, and bring that melon up to the house," Dad said. What we had not known was Dad had bought a melon from Old Man Hoover and hid it in the spring to cool overnight. We whooped and hollered all the way to the house. Mom had the butcher knife, spoons, and saltshaker out on the porch when we got there. That melon tasted just about as close to heaven as we boys could imagine.

Mom's yard was bare of grass; she kept it swept clean. She had made little circles of rocks and planted zinnias in some of the beds. The flowers bloomed bright yellow, red, purple, with a scattering of white mixed in. They were a glorious island of color in the clean swept yard. Some beds held 'Four O'clock' that smelled like a baby's breath. All of these flowers were watered with buckets of used water from the kitchen and washhouse. Mom kept a broom on the porch to chase us boys if we stepped in a flowerbed.

"You boys do the chores while Mom finishes supper. I will do the milking tonight." Doing the chores was another day's work. We shucked corn for the hogs, and carried plenty of water from the well for them to drink and wallow in. We gathered the eggs from the hen house and made sure the chickens had feed and water for tomorrow. We carried bales of hay from the barn for the horses, and gave each one a coffee can of oats. The yearlings in the little pasture got a bale of hay, some cracked corn, and had their water replenished. All this made a great sauce for our supper.

After supper, we all went out on the gallery to rest and talk of the world and all that was in it. The sun had fallen below the horizon, and the land was enveloped in the glow of the evening. Dad told of important things he had read in the Grit newspaper. He pointed out the stars of the night to us boys. "There is the big dipper. See how it points to Polaris? Cassiopeia is directly opposite from the dipper. The south sky is filled with Scorpio." I am not sure us boys paid him much attention at the time, but I now remember. Mom sat in her rocker and hummed her favorite church hymns. She coaxed the girls to sing along with her. Their music filled the night air with a melody that rivaled the night birds calls. In fact, the bobwhite quail, nighthawk, and whip-poor-will seemed to join in the singing of the girls. That was all a world ago...but seems to be just a few yesterdays. Perhaps it was.

How to Build the Perfect Front Porch

Greetings from Alice's front porch here in our hometown. There is a new look to everything; it is green. It is amazing how fast the brown grass of just a few weeks ago awakens and sports a beautiful coat of green. My flowers have even decided to brave the hot summer and bloom anyway. Perhaps with all the grass the deer will leave our garden alone. And we have a new greeting. It is no longer, "Good morning," it is, "How much rain did you get?" I have had all kinds of answers. Some say they have received two and six-tenths, others report they have gotten two and three quarter inches of rain. I am pleased to report we have gotten a little over three inches, and the clouds are still rumbling all around. See there, the first storyteller hasn't a chance.

Gilbert Vickers and I were talking and he said, "You know, I think sitting on the gallery watching it rain is about the best medicine a fellow can have." I agreed with Gilbert. John and Diane Yarbrough live west of town, off County Road 288, with a front porch that faces east. John and Diane's house sits on a hill with a view of 360 degrees. A gentle slope to the north gives them a spectacular sight of approaching clouds. John said, "We built our house with that in mind. We often sit there, have coffee and watch the sun come up." With all the recent rain, John said his land turned emerald green overnight.

There is another advantage to the rains we have had; they fell slowly, over an extended weeks' time. Had we gotten all the rain at one time, most of it would have run off. When rain runs down the driveway, it spills into the little creek at the foot of the hill. From there it is gone, for our use, all the way to the ocean. I suppose the fishes in the sea need a drink also.

John, Gilbert and I got to talking about how to build the best front porch for sitting and watching the world turn, and the rain fall. We decided the porch should face the east. "That gives you a nice view of the sunrise, and it is in total shade in the evening," John said. He went on to suggest, "The ceiling needs to be insulated to keep you cooler while sitting there." I countered with; "But John, I want to hear the rain falling on the tin roof." Gilbert agreed with me. John suggested the porch should be at least 12 feet wide and as long as possible. We all agreed. Several fans and lights would be nice. We became silent. Our minds had exhausted the subject, and the only thing left to do was wander off. We did.

About dark it occurred to me, we had missed one important item for our ultimate front porch. Every porch needs a swing, big enough for two, with chains that squeak. That way Alice can sit with our grandchildren, and tell them stories of when she was a little girl, and it rained for weeks and weeks.

Just Singing, Singing in the Rain

Do you ever get a song stuck in your head? You know, it comes into your head as you are busy with the chores of your day and you hum a few lines of the song. Then it becomes a challenge to remember the words. It is exciting to find you do remember the words. They have been waiting, buried somewhere in the recesses of your mind. Songs like "Old Dan Tucker," or "Yankee Doodle Dandy," just pop up without notice, and you sing them. Some of the songs are the sophisticated little ditties like, "Three Blind Mice."   Quite often, it may be a Broadway melody like "Somewhere Over the Rainbow" or "On the Street Where You Live" you remember. And you sing it...all day long. And you can't stop singing it. You have gotten the song hung on the barbs of you mind and there is no getting it unhooked. It is a lovely song, and you enjoy it...but all day long? You are bitten by the bug infecting you with "Clogged Cranium Disorder," or as the media would say, "CCD."

A more advanced malady is the case where the bitten singer can't remember all the words. He sings a few lines then trails off into an unintelligible jumble of words and notes. That is called, "CCDUJ." Greg, our son, remembers riding to work with me, and hearing me struggle with bits of songs like: "Deep within my heart lies a melody......," and "Mares eat oats, bears eat oats, and little lambs eat ivy. I'd eat ivy too, wouldn't you?....." That must have driven him up the wall of the pickup cab. It bothered me too.

Recently I have a little song that has lodged in my mind. It refuses to move. All day long, the thing just grins and keeps me singing, and singing. I know all the words, and a close feel for the tune, but I can't seem to dislodge it. The song is "Blue Tailed Fly." I think Burl Ives made it popular when I was a youngster. The working men sang this old traditional song in the fields and workshops of early America. Thank goodness I don't have the advanced symptoms of CCD, for I know all the words. And I am going to share them with you.

The Blue-tailed Fly

When I was young, I used to wait on my master and pass him his plate, and hand him the bottle when he got dry, and brush away the blue-tailed fly.

(Chorus)

Jimmy cracked corn, and I don't care, Jimmy cracked corn and I don't care, my master has gone away.

One day he rode around the farm, the flies so numerous they did swarm. One chanced to bite him on the thigh, the Devil take the blue-tailed fly.

(Chorus)

The horse he bucked and he pitched. He threw my Master right in the ditch. He died and the jury wondered why; the verdict was the Blue-tailed Fly.

(Chorus)

Now we buried him neth the simmon tree. His epitaph is there to see; beneath this stone I am doomed to lie, all cause of the Blue-tailed fly.

This little song just hangs on. It has been hung there for two days, and it is getting a little old. It is not a bad song, I just want it to go away. So I called the doctor. He said, "Take two aspirins, and call me in the morning."

Fancy Boots and Pretty Music Go Together

Some Sundays are more special than others. Like this past Sunday for instance. John Yarbrough and I looked up and saw John Steel come in the front door of the church. He took the program Alice offered, smiled his shy smile and eased into the sanctuary. John and I both looked up at the roof and eased toward the door. After we were convinced, the celling was not going to fall we went to welcome John.

John's lean body fit well in a white western shirt with pearl buttons, and cinched down with a string tie. His browned, deep lined leather face sported that grin for which he is famous. A modest belt held up a pair of Levis that were starched and ironed. John stuffed the blue jeans into the tops of his boots, as if to say "Yep, they are handmade and I like the color and cut of the tops."

We welcomed him, and helped him find a seat somewhere in the middle of the church. We figured there he would not be a bother to anyone, and nobody would bother him. John and I exchanged questioning glances, for we could not remember ever seeing John Steel in church.

The singing went well. The song leader picked out all the old favorite hymns of the church and Pat, the pianist, added all the runs and trills in just the right places. I noticed John had picked up a hymnal and was singing along with the congregation. His baritone voice swelled and filled the sanctuary with a glorious sound. Soon those of us close by stopped singing and just listened. He continued singing all the hymns with his magnificent voice. Most of the congregation fell silent and let the song leader, Pat, and John Steel fill our hearts with inspiration.

Then the preacher launched his sermon. He passed several chances to stop preaching, but pulled back and made another run at quitting. He finally found a decent spot, slowed, and came to a full stop. I am not sure many heard much of the sermon for we were still marveling at John's beautiful voice. We all wanted to shake John's hand and tell him what a beautiful voice he had.

I asked John where he learned to sing like that. "Out in Coleman, Texas. A boot maker named Tex Robin and me had a group that went around singing at churches. We had a great time, but his boot making got in the way and we had to stop," he said. "In fact Tex made these boots I am wearing more than 20 years ago. They were as pretty as his voice.

Alice invited him to dinner, but he declined. "Thanks Mrs. Alice. I have a cow about to calve and I need to check on her.

Voting Advice

When I get confused, which is often these days, I go see John Steel. With all these newspaper ads, television ads, internet ads, and most annoying telephone ads urging me to vote for some handsome man or beautiful woman, I need help. They all look so honest, and upstanding I can't believe they would make a law that would be detrimental to our society.

I drove up to John's sagging gate, got out, drug it open, drove through, got out and closed it. I could hear that spotted dog of John's barking alerting his master he had company. The dusty road to his little shotgun house was a pleasure to drive: ruts, rocks, and sharp turns shook my old pick up to its rusty frame. I hollered, started to get out then thought maybe I better let John call his dog off first. John ambled out on the porch with a cup of coffee in his hand and a smile on his leathered face, shouted the dog to shut up.

"Get out Baker: he won't bite." I have heard that before, and I have learned to be a little slow getting out at country houses.

We sat on the porch quietly surveying nature and the beautiful morning. I nursed my cup of twice boiled coffee, trying to get a little of it down. I knew better than to rush my need for information. That would come in John's own time.

We looked at his garden, his new calf, and the chicken yard. The hens were a motley group of happy girls. All colors of chickens filled the yard, herded around by a speckled rooster. "Remind me to give you a dozen eggs before you leave," John said. I made a mental note of that promise.

Back on the front porch, with yet another cup of dark brew, John finely asked the question, "What are you doing out in these parts of the woods?" I shared my dilemma with him. John listened with patience. I rambled on and on, listing all my questions, fears, and doubts. "I don't know any of these guys running for office. I don't know their work ethics. I don't know their past or their plans for our future. How am I going to make a proper decision?"

"Well, Baker, it's a little like that chicken yard out there by the barn. That Dominicker rooster spends his day preening himself so he looks good. He stands tall and erect, struts around the yard, eating grain and even laying mash all day. His 'work day' consists of crowing a few times, usually not on time with any clock, and chasing the girls around the yard. He doesn't lay eggs, hatch chicks, and can't tell time. What he promises to give us, he has to take from us in advance," he said.

I waited for him to tell me what to do about my problem. He just poured another cup of coffee, and gazed off into the morning sun.

"Well, John, that is the truth, but what can I do about making a decision about voting for one of them?" I asked. John sipped his coffee, thought a few moments then said,

"Baker, I suggest you tack their ads on the barn door, toss a dart at the lot of them and vote for the one you hit."

I got my promised eggs and drove home a little disappointed. John's advice seemed a little bit shallow. My dilemma still hounded me. Upon reflection I decided perhaps he is right. It may be John has put his finger on the solution. His advice is about the only one we have in our society today. Now, where can I find a good sharp dart?

Friendship

We met Bryan and Shelia Evans at Gatwick airport more than thirty years ago. We were coming home: they were going to Texas for the first time. We were excited for we were homesick. They were excited for this was a dream coming true for them. Brian has been a great fan of Texas and all things Texan all his life. He thought he had just met a "Real Texas Cattle Baron." I didn't have the heart to tell him I was all boots and no cows. We have corresponded all these years, and I am not sure I have ever confessed to him the truth. They were flying to Dallas and we were on our way to Austin. Something clicked and we bonded immediately. I figured it was my natural good looks and handsome carriage. Alice suggested it might be because I was wearing my Stetson hat right there in the middle of "Jolly olde England." The ugly Texan if there ever was one. We visited on the flight all the way home. I suggested while they were in Texas they should visit us.

They did. Alice met them at the door with the offer of tea. Bryan quickly said, "That would be lovely." He was expecting a brewed cup of hot tea: what Alice served was a tall glass of iced tea. However, Brian gracefully said nothing. I am not sure he knew what to do with all that ice swimming in his 'cup of tea.' We served them brisket Bar-B-Q, pinto beans, and all the trimmings we have come to enjoy here in Texas. I am sure it looked strange to them, and perhaps tasted even stranger, but they kept the stiff upper lip and worked through. We spent the evening in the back yard exchanging stories and jokes until the wee hours.

They insisted we visit them in England. We did. Those folks know how to entertain two naive Texas kids. One of the interesting sights they took us to see was a joisting tournament at Belvoir Castle. It was exciting to see two armored knights, mounted on great steeds, carrying 12 foot lances racing in a full gallop toward each other. Lances were splintered, shields knocked loose, and men tumbled to the turf. I don't think I have ever witnessed anything like that back on the ranch. We retired to a Pub, named "Yea Olde Trip to Jerusalem," claiming to be the oldest Pub in all of England. It has been a Pub since 1189. However the ale was fresh, and as cool a drink as you will find in the 'Mother Land.'

Newstead Abby, built in 1163 by Henry II as a penitence for having had Thomas Beckett killed, was our next visit. During Henry VIII's reign, the abbey was given to the King's friends where it fell into disuse, and ruin. We know it as Lord Bryon's home. It is a handsome structure with grand landscaping and pleasant walkways. A manmade lake enhances the idyllic setting. In a small garden, a headstone reads in part...

Here lie the bones of one

Who possessed Beauty

Without Vanity,

Strength without Insolence,

Courage without Ferocity

And all the Virtues of Man

Without his Vices

Brian explained this is where Lord Bryon laid his favorite dog, Boatswain, when he died.

Our host kept us entertained with so much to see and do; it was hard to keep them all in perspective. We visited D.H. Lawrence's home, ate fish and chips, standing on the sidewalk in the shade of those grand old sycamore trees, and made a 'walk-about' in the countryside. Brian and Shelia took us to their favorite Pub for dinner. It indeed was a public house, with darts, cards, and a game of skittles out back. One of the card games had an unusual twist. If you needed a card, but didn't have it, you could say, "I imagine the King of Hearts, or whatever card you needed, and it counted as if it were there. I can think of several times that would be handy.

As you can see, friends can be found most anywhere. Some are just passing fancies; others become golden jewels, to be treasured forever. That is how we feel about Brian and Shelia Evans.

Striking While the Iron is Hot

I don't know why, but men have the habit of walking around town hatching ideas. Women are not burdened with that problem: but men sure are. The older we become the more we give birth to new ideas. Like the time I had the bright idea of Liberty Hill becoming the TV Advertising Capitol of the world. You know, filming cars and trucks splashing through water, and carrying great loads of logs and everything. That idea came, lived a short time, and then had an ignoble death. Or how about the time I had the idea to get one of the space shuttles set up down at the Lions Park? Man, that would draw the crowds to Liberty Hill big time. You know that idea didn't hatch either. Once I had an idea of building a mountain in the area. I could just see a towering mountain with trees, and bushes, and maybe snow on the peak. People would come for miles around just to marvel at the site. They could practice their mountain climbing and hiking, and all having a great time. That idea fizzled also. We could not find enough loose dirt to build "Mt. Liberty Hill."

Bull Durham, Camels, and Brown Mule

Some things we are just born to endure. Freckles come to mind. Straw for hair is another. In my case, at about 14 years old, I discovered I had two left feet. In fact, I still have two left feet. Alice has been kind and long-suffering in not reminding me of that deficiency. Most of the time I am able to get down the street fairly well without falling down or stumbling into something expensive.

However, our society often manages to entangle us into actions that are difficult or even harmful. One that comes to mind is new shoes. You know the minute you force your feet into a pair of shiny black dress shoes you have a problem. Blisters begin to appear before you have hobbled two blocks. And in the long run, you know a corn is growing on that little toe. For little kids a new Sunday suit is a fountainhead of itch. It never goes away. Not only is it uncomfortable, we felt silly wearing it. Why can't we wear our stripped overalls to church? Lucky for youngsters today the Sunday suit has about disappeared. In fact, this trend may have gone just about, as far as the pendulum can swing.

Another social habit we were born into was tobacco. My grandfather smoked a pipe. It smelled strong enough to walk. I am not sure it didn't. To me I imagined he whistled and the pipe and a can of Prince Albert tobacco would appear. He stuffed the bowl with the brown stuff, and lit it with a live coal from the fireplace. Or if it was summer time, he used a kitchen match, lit by striking it on a brass button on his overalls. In those days everyone who had reached what he considered grown, used tobacco. Grandma usually used Tuberose snuff, but only in the privacy of her sewing room. Many of the tough old men chewed a plug of tobacco called Brown Mule. It should have been called Black Mule for its color and smell. The worst offenders were the uncles of the family. The bigger the man, the blacker the cigar he smoked. What the uncles seemed to delight in was getting the ladies and us kids into a small room and lighting up a cigar. The air became blue with smoke and the floor covered with ash.

The desire to smoke came upon us boys at an early age. If we could sneak a handful of matches, and a packet of dad's cigarette papers, we would go down on the creek and smoke cedar bark. It lit easy, produced plenty of smoke, and burned our tongues something fierce. We talked big, and puffed with abandon. We could hardly wait until we were old enough to buy a sack of Bull Durham tobacco. It came with a packet of papers to roll our own. Someday, we bragged, we would buy a pack of 'ready rolls,' and sure enough be big boys on the block. I championed Chesterfields because the pack looked so neat. The older boys thought the Lucky Strikes and Camels were the only way to smoke.

However, things do change, and sometimes for the better. Smoking is on the way out, and good riddance. Cities have banned smoking in businesses. It is not a cool thing anymore. The world smells better with tobacco's demise. There are still a few old folks that cling to the habit, but they are going fast. This may be a problem for the cigarette manufacturers, and the state of Kentucky. However, I can see them, with their deep pockets, making baseball caps, or satin bicycle racing pants, or football helmets, and making a fortune.

Of course, that still leaves me with freckles, straw hair, and two left feet.

Some Roads Take a Long Time to Travel

This last weekend Alice and I, and our friends from Lubbock, Lonnie and Nancy Hollingsworth, drove to Fredericksburg to see the wild flowers. Some trip. Some flowers. After last summer's heat and drought, Mother Nature has outdone herself with a glorious display of spring beauty. The roadsides are streaked with bluebonnets where there was none last year. Patches of bright yellow flowers that Lady Bird Johnson called DYCs were plentiful. We stopped at the Wild Seed Farm and admired their display of fields of corn poppies. The colors are so bright and luxuriant it fairly astounds you. Traveling north on Texas Highway 16 towards Llano is a delight to see. Along the roadway, many fields are splashed with abundant white mallows and prickly poppies. The pastures looked like a freak snow storm had passed that way. Indian Paint brush, purple holly hawk, and bee balm were scattered throughout the drive. Willow City Loop is a delight to drive. The county road, making its way through the mountains, hills, and valleys is a lovely drive any day of the year, but covered with poppies and bluebonnets it is awesome.

We drove back to Fredericksburg for lunch. Linden House is one of those restaurants that features a real German menu. The building was constructed 130 years ago and it gives you the feeling of dining on the Rhine. The waitresses probably were speaking English, but I could not understand a word they said, nor could I read the menu. So I just pointed to a dish, ordered, and it was delicious. Bratwurst sausage, sweet potato salad, and pickled beets are feast for a king. Sitting on one of the many benches along the busy street we saw the human condition walk by. Old ladies, dressed to the nines, waddling fat men dressed in Nike's and silly shorts, and red necked drug store cowboys paraded by in a steady stream.

Lonnie and I got to talking about how long we had known each other. Alice and Nancy were quick to do the math for us: 57 years they said. Fifty-seven years; unbelievable.

I was in the University of Texas. We lived in Breckenridge Apartments student housing on Lake Austin Boulevard. Our next-door neighbor was Fred Snyder, from North Carolina. He liked to fish. We often got our fishing gear, along with a can of worms, and headed for the river just below Tom Miller Dam. That day Fred had invited his friend, Lonnie Hollingsworth, a pharmacy student, to go with us. Lonnie and I sat on a boulder at the water's edge and talked of cabbages and kings, and a world of things, never bothering the worms or fish. Fred caught enough fish for us to take home to Alice to cook for our supper. So began a wonderful friendship.

We have made trips to the piney woods of East Texas, and enjoyed the world of azaleas. We have waded in the surf at Corpus Christie, and climbed the mountains of West Texas. We enjoyed seeing "Sound of Music" on stage in London where Lonnie sang along with the cast, and we didn't get booted out. We have played marbles in the sand, and watched football in the stadium; there is not much we haven't done or seen. He claims he has seen an inch of rain once, and it was too muddy to drink and too wet to plow. I think we are good for another 57 years.

Climbing Into Our Playhouse in the Sky

Dad's windmill and water tank was our playhouse. The tank was mounted eight feet above ground on four-cedar posts. There was just enough of the platform outside the tank for us to creep around the edge. At times it became our palace, and we could survey our kingdom and all that was in it from its height. The cool water in the tank felt good on hot summer days. Beneath it, in the shade of the water tank, we played as if we were in our royal court. Occasionally the water tower became our impregnable castle. From its ramparts, we defended it from all manner of assaults. It was exciting to push the scaling ladders of the invading hordes away from the embattlements and watch the enemy fall to the ground in screaming heaps. One of our weapons of defense was boiling oil. We kept a pot, heated to a smoking degree, ready to dump upon the hapless masses below. Their screams of pain were a joy to our cruel little hearts.

Often Dad shouted, "While you guys are up there, see how much water is in the tank." That would interrupt our play of castle and palace. Poof! There went our make-believe world. However, it was another challenge climbing further up to the inspection opening at the top, and report the level of water in the castle... I mean tank.

The real thrill was playing on the 30-foot steel tower that held the great windmill fan. The blades caught the ever-present breeze, turned the fan round and round at a dizzying speed. The gears groaned lifting the sucker rods, which clanked against the standpipe, creating an unearthly sound. The cool water rose in the standpipe and flowed into the water tank.

Climbing the steel tower was a test of nerves. At the top of the tower, where the four corners of the tower came together was a two foot square platform for workmen to service the air motor. Our goal was to mount that workspace and keep from being knocked off by the whirling fan. Only one boy could be on the tower at a time, making the act like a dare devil's show. Encouragement and taunts were shouted from far below. "Go on, you can make it." "Don't be a sissy, climb higher." Those were the times when I first faced fear. The height, the sound, the tower's vibrations all became a monster taunting a little boy. The thrill of coming down was a reward from enduring the fear. Reaching over from the ladder and grabbing the standpipe required skill and nerve. But, sliding down the 30-foot standpipe was a delight worth the climb. How great the earth felt to my feet was a part of the fun. I don't remember any boy being knocked off the service platform. Some of the 'big ole boys' made it all the way to the top of the tower and reported they could see all the way to the next town. I took their word for it.

On summer nights, sleeping with the windows open, the sounds of the fan turning, the gears grinding, the sucker rods banging, and the water splashing into the tank lulled me to a peaceful sleep. I kind of miss that time. However I don't intend to try to climb another tower.

True Fishing Stories Are Hard to Find.

Spring is just around the corner. The wild plum trees are in full bloom and filling the air with their lovely perfume. The meadows are vibrant green with new spring grass and budding flowers. The open spaces are crowded with anomies, which have the unusual trick of being mostly white with a few purple and occasional pink blossoms. The blue bonnets are lifting their heads and are about to burst into their bright blue flowers that will cover the hillsides. This year promises to be a glorious, colorful spring here in Central Texas.

However, spring brings out a different urge in old men besides admiring the flowers. Fishing. If you spot a gaggle of old men drinking coffee at some watering hole, like the Exxon station, odds are the talk is about fish they have caught, or fish they are planning to catch. One of the area's best fishermen I have ever met is Randal Fletcher. He has fished rivers, lakes, creeks, and ponds from Amarillo to Brownsville and from Texarkana to El Paso. And he comes home with his icebox full. His favorite spot to fish is Matagorda, on the coast where the Colorado River empties into the Gulf of Mexico. That great expanse of blue skies and green water is inspiring to see, and the water is teaming with all kinds of fish. However, just a few weeks ago, Randal tells me he caught plenty of blue catfish on Lake Travis. He likes to fish by tying a line and baited hook to a float, which he calls 'jug fishing.' The baited hook needs to be about one foot from the bottom. He feels that is just about right to catch the bigger cats. Randal says he likes to fish for yellow cats, but likes eating blue cats better.

"What is the biggest cat fish you have caught, Randal?" I asked. He sidestepped that question by telling me about two of his buddies, Bob Brooks and Slim Marshall, who caught a 57-pound yellow catfish at the slab over in Llano County. Randal went on to tell me of an old man who said he caught a big yellow catfish out of Jenks Branch long, long ago. "How big was he?" Randal asked. The old man did not know how big he was. "Well, how much did he weigh?" Randal insisted. "Well, mister Randal, he was so big his eyes were the size of a horse's eye," he said.

Randal told of a fisherman who was out on the river in his little boat minding his line when a snake with a frog in his mouth swam by. He felt sorry for the frog so he netted the pair and turned the frog loose. Then he felt sorry for the snake. He held the snake just behind the head and gave him a shot of whiskey he just happened to have, then tossed him into the water. Soon he heard a banging on the side of his boat. Looking over the side, he saw the same snake, this time with two frogs in his mouth.

A few years ago, Randal and two buddies were flounder fishing at Matagorda. They filled their sacks with those tasty flat fish and decided to look for bigger game the next day. They cut up bait, loaded their equipment into a 16-foot fishing boat and went out into the Gulf about 15 or 20 miles. Soon one of them hooked a shark. It gave them a royal battle, but they managed to land that 9-foot fish into their 16-foot boat. With three big men and a nine-foot shark, the boat was full. In fact it was overflowing, and they considered giving the boat, fishing gear, and equipment to the flopping monster. Randal finally was able to dispatch the shark with a whack on the head with a paddle.

Randal said the shark tasted good, but it was no match for the flounder. The fish were seasoned, rolled in corn meal, fried in deep peanut oil, and served on a strip of brown paper. Now how is that for a modest angler telling a true fishing story?

Revolutions Come and Go

This weekend our son Gordon and I went to a Buggy Whip Manufacturing convention held in Gary Martin's shop, in way far South Austin. As you might guess, it really wasn't a Buggy Whip Manufacturing convention. That is just what I called it.

I grew up hand lettering signs. We painted all the signs the public saw with a brush and a can of paint. We painted roadside billboards that measured 14 feet by 48 feet, hanging from a walk board, with cans of paint and a fistful of brushes. We painted little one foot by two-foot signs with the same paint and a few smaller brushes. In addition, we lettered company names on cars and trucks the same way.

Then came the revolution. The digital revolution. Now we produce all those signs with the aid of a computer and printer. What a relief. No little brushes and cans of paint are necessary, just punch a few keys on a computer and *presto,* a sign appears as if by magic. So I came to call hand-lettered signs the Buggy Whip Industry. There are few calls for buggy whips these days.

I was wrong. There is a strong demand for the old hand painted signs I grew up making. Many national chains of restaurants demand all their signs to be hand lettered. Chuy's Mexican Café, Salt Grass Steak House, Torchy's Tacos,

Longhorn Steak House, Schlotzskys and many others use hand lettered signs. Many of the amusement parks such as Six Flags have all their signs hand-lettered. So I guess I will have to take back the idea that the art of hand-lettered signs is anything like making buggy whips. The industry is alive and well.

Gary Martin Signs is one of those shops that specialize in producing the unique work of art; hand painted signs. This weekend Gary opened his shop to his trade friends for a convocation of hand painted signs for the Guys and Gals. Gary's shop is a bouquet of smells, sights, and sounds. The rich smell of linseed oil greets the visitors at the door. The different colors, with their pigments, create a delight for the eyes. The blaze of colors on signs finished and those being painted remind you of the leaves of fall. The walls of the shop are plastered with old works, posters, and graffiti from long ago. The sound of saws, hammers, and pleasant banter is comforting to the ear.

Big Mike from Minnesota came to regale us with his stories and show us his 'hot licks' with his brush. His drooping mustache, crew cut hair, and bright smile entertained all. George, of Albuquerque, amazed the group with samples of his sign art and photography. He was a bundle of energy and good cheer. Derrick from California is a hardworking, fast learning protégé of Mike's. Austin's own Greg, Gary, Evan and Theresa shared with the group their own sign art.

With all that talent and skill in one shop, in South Austin, they could probably make you a buggy whip...if you really want one. I know they could paint one on your kitchen wall if that would help.

To Reach Your Goal Takes a Little Grit.

Little kids in little town are always looking for a way to make money. We quickly learned picking up discarded pop bottles alongside of the highways would bring cash money of two cents each. It only took three bottles and you could purchase a cold Pepsi Cola and a penny piece of candy. That worked well during the hot dry summer days, but on cold wet days scavenging pop bottles was a little difficult. Mowing grass was a popular moneymaker for us boys during the summer. Mrs. Elliot had me mow, trim, and rake her yard and I got paid 25 cents. I felt I had become a tycoon businessman. That 25 cents bought a ticket to the BurnTex picture show, plus a bag of popcorn. That left a few cents for tomorrow's buying adventure. Of course, that job lasted only until summer faded into fall and dead grass. What we needed was a winter money-making project. The old men hanging around the feed store were always talking about trapping for fur-bearing animals. They said a fox pelt would bring four or five dollars, and a ring tail pelt brought, sometimes, eight dollars. That sounded great to us. We borrowed a few steel traps and set them in a line across Mr. Wingren's pasture. All we caught in our line of traps that winter was one rat, two possums, a skunk and one dog. The dog was the worst problem. We had to get one of the big Shillings' boys to get him loose from the trap. Our total take for the trapping season was ten cents for the two possum hides and a nickel for the skunk pelt.

One of our gang was smarter than the rest of us. James Smith was a small kid, and was not as handsome as we were, but he was a go getter. He found an ad in a magazine extolling the merits of becoming a sales person and delivery man for the newspaper *Grit*. He sent off for the information and was soon selling the paper to subscribers and folks up and down the street for ten cents a copy, every week, rain or shine. He earned four cents a copy for each one he sold. It was not hard for us to see his fortune piling up. He might have to open an account at the First State Bank. He did well, and we were all proud of him for his enterprising business smarts. The rest of us had to do with the odd jobs we could find.

I got to thinking about that newspaper. I wonder if it was still around. I looked it up in my set of Funk and Wagnall Encyclopedias. You will be pleased the paper is still being published, it's now a magazine. The publication is still directed to the rural and small town folks and is successful. The paper was started in the late 1800's by a German immigrant, Dietrick Lamare. By the 1930's the paper had a circulation of a half million. The paper ran 40 pages and had all kinds of information for the subscribers. The paper had sections for news, women, family, story, and comics. The comics caught my attention. They ran the comics, Blondie, Dixie Dugan, Donald

Duck, Flash Gordon, Joe Palooka, Jungle Jim, The Lone Ranger, Out Our Way, and my favorite, Prince Valliant. You can see the paper had something in it for everyone. Lamare's success was in part attributed to his vision for the paper. His policy for the paper was;

> "Always keep *Grit* from being pessimistic. Avoid printing those things which distort the minds of readers or make them feel at odds with the world. Avoid showing the wrong side of things, or making people feel discontented. Do nothing that will encourage fear, worry, or temptation. Wherever possible, suggest peace and good will toward men. Give our readers courage and strength for their daily tasks. Put happy thoughts, cheer, and contentment into their hearts."

Well, we all needed a little *Grit* in our lives in those days. However, most of us found something that worked. I hope James Smith is still selling *Grit* and doing well.

Do You Ever Feel Like You've Been Snookered?

Through the years, Alice has been my cheerleader. She has always blown blue smoke my way. She has always supported my many dead-end projects as if she thought they would create a better world. I have enjoyed the backing. Can you imagine my surprise when the other day she said, "Hollis, I am a little disappointed with you." That cut deep, and I snuck away into a dark corner to lick my wound. I thought, "Haven't I supplied her with a nice car for her to drive?" Well, I realize the air in the tires, and the ever-empty gas tank are still mine. I try to keep the car washed and waxed, and vacuumed. But she is disappointed. And the house is a cleverly designed warm-in-winter-and-cools-in- summer abode for her to use. Sure, the floors, windows, and garbage are still mine, but the house is hers. But she is disappointed. Alice doesn't claim the yard. It belongs to me. I mow the grass, plant and water the flowers. I get to trim the bushes and trees. However, I do it all just so she can enjoy the beauty and reap the admiration of her guests. But she is disappointed with me.

I crept back into the house and asked, "Why are you so disappointed with me?" Really, deep down in the recesses of my being I am a nice guy. I feared her answer. The answer was not long in coming.

"You have been going to Lions Club meetings for months, enjoying their hospitality, eating their food, and have not joined the organization," she said.

"Well, they asked me to visit them and have breakfast with them, and be their guest. And besides, they serve great food," I replied.

"Well the next time you go to mooch food from the hard working folks at the Lions Club, you ask for an application to join. I will fill it out for you," Alice said.

I crawled back into my hole to contemplate the status of my life. The only thing I could think of was a quote by Groucho Marx; "I don't want to join a club that would put up with the likes of me." Alice and someone at the Lions Club think I am OK. The clouds began to clear and reveal the brilliant sunshine. I swear I heard a blue bird singing. A gentle, warm breeze invaded my space. Maybe Groucho was wrong. Maybe he was just having a bad day. Yes, that is what it was. I crawled from my hidey-hole and ran back to the house, and told Alice I would make her proud of me again: I would join the club.

Then another quote crept into my conscience. A quote from Jim Linz. A quote from long ago when the world was at ease, "Be careful with a man who buys his printing ink by the barrel." I think I can handle that.

Feeding Cattle

Dry cold winter days on the ranch can be a real chore. It is especially so if all of the summer, grass is gone and the winter grass is scarce. Those cows can get a little lean and hungry. But if you live here in central Texas, you probably have plenty of prickly pear on the ranch. That has saved many ranchers and their livestock.

The day was crispy cold with a gentle north breeze. I decided I had better check on John Steel. I drove up to his little shotgun house and that spotted dog didn't run out to eat my leg off. I saw John's battered pickup parked under the Live Oak tree near the yard fence, so I knew he was not far away. I beeped my horn, but got no answer. I listened carefully and made out a roaring sound from out in the pasture. I moseyed out that way. There John was, burning pear for his little bunch of cows. The spotted dog came to meet me, but the cows did not look up. They just kept eating with gusto the freshly burned pear leaves. John noticed he had company, and he shut down his flame throwing, thorn burning, propane pear burner. "About time for a cup of coffee," he said.

Back at the house, John put another stick of wood in the kitchen stove. I knew then we were in for warmed over breakfast coffee. It was plenty strong, a bit bitter, but hot. I knew he liked it that way. I pretended to agree. We sat around the stove in his two rawhide bottomed straight-backed chairs, and sipped the black brew. I said, "John , tell me about burning pear."

"When I was just a kid Dad and I burned pear one winter from November until spring grass finally came up," he said. "We would hitch the mules to the wagon and go over to the Howard place and get a load of pear. We'd done burned all of ours. We cut the leaves off the plant with a long handled ax and loaded them on the wagon with a pitchfork. We'd bring them home, build a brush fire, and burn all the stickers off the pear leaves and feed them to the cows. They sure loved those green, juicy pear leaves. It took from 50 to a 100 leaves to fill up one cow, so you can see it was a lot of work feeding all the stock. Then we got a kerosene-fired pear burner. Man, was that a relief. It was a tank that held a few gallons of fuel with a harness to carry it on your back. We pumped it up with a tire pump to give it pressure. It had a long pipe with a burner on the end so you could walk around a pear plant and burn all the stickers off real easy."

We walked out to the barn and he showed me the old kerosene pear burner hanging from a nail on the wall. "We got through that winter with that old burner," he said.

"What kind of a burner are you using now to get the stickers off the pear leaves," I asked.

"A few years after the kerosene burner came out, Dad heard of a new kind. He found it advertised in the Sears and

Roebuck catalogue, and he ordered one. Now that was a honey. It used propane for fuel and you didn't have to pump it up, nor carry on you back. It had a long hose you just dragged behind you from the tank. It rarely gave you the trouble the old kerosene burner did," he said. We finished that pot of black stuff he called coffee and he went back to burning pear stickers.

I talked to my cousin Barney Baker, who lives on the home place, way up Morgan Creek in Burnet County. Said he was burning pear himself these days. It is not cold but it sure is dry. He burns pear most of the day and then puts out range cubes for the cows to supplement their diet. His cows are doing well, and the market is good for the ranchers. "You can borrow my pickup, or my shot gun, but you can't borrow my pear burner," he said.

Plowing Grandma's Garden

About this time of year, Grandma always wanted the garden plowed. She liked getting the onions, cabbage, and cauliflower planted early. Plowing the garden was the easy part; cleaning the cow lot, and spreading it on the garden was the hard part. "Now Hollis, you go get Pete from the pasture and get the garden plowed," she said. Grandma's request was my command. With a few nubbins of corn from the crib in my pocket, I went into the pasture to find Pete and the other horses. I swear they could hear Grandma's orders and hide in the thickest brush they could find those mornings. Pete had a bell around his neck that rang as he grazed the winter grass. He was 16 hands tall, grey with specks of white on his rump; he was not an appaloosa but I called him one. However, most mornings, with his sixth sense, he would stand still not allowing the bell to sound and make me hunt him. I called the horses to no avail. I then shucked the corn nubbins with as much noise as I could, and they moved out of the brush to get a bite of the grain, knowing a coffee can of oats awaited them at the barn.

I fear I would have trouble harnessing Pete to the plow that day. I remember you needed to put the bit and bridle, with blinders, on first. The collar and hames, with all its' loops, rings, and fasteners, followed. You needed to fasten the girt around the horse's belly, but not too tight. Attaching the trace chains to the singletree on the plow came next, then threading the reins through the loops and brackets completed the harnessing. That is the way I remember the task.

Grandma insisted I plough east and west across last year's rows, then bed the garden rows north and south. Looked to me the cabbages wouldn't care which way the rows went, but she was adamant.

Pete was good at his job and he leaned into the collar with a willing spirit. When we ploughed to the far end of the garden, it was no trouble for him to turn around and fall into the next row. However as we finished the row nearest the barn, I had to be strong to turn him around and plough away from home. When we finished the day's work, I would unhitch the trace chains from the singletree and lay them across Pete's back. He then let me climb upon him and we headed for home. I liked riding up there. The leather harness smelled good with sweat, and the chains jangled with a haunting melody. For those few hundred yards, I was 'King of my Domain.'

This past week our son Greg and I worked our garden. It is much smaller than Grandma's garden, only six raised beds 20 feet long, but they produce well. And we have fewer to feed from our garden. We just cranked up our Troy Built tiller, I call Pete, and in a few passes, the garden is ready for cabbage. I wish Grandma were here to help do the planting.

The Quadrantid Shooting Stars Return

Our son Gordon had a paper route in our neighborhood sometime in the middle 1960's. Many of his friends threw the early morning routes nearby. They would get the papers about four o'clock in the morning, load their bicycles, and start peddling their appointed areas. Of course, there were clicks of paperboys vying with each other to see who could scare the others the most. Jumping from shrubbery and yelling was a favorite tactic that caused a lot of excitement with little harm. Tossed water balloons were effective also but did not help the condition of the papers. The fun, as always, escalated into an early morning mini-war of nerves and near misses. Thrown stones became the missile of choice. Luckily, none of the young men were hurt badly, just bicycle dents and broken spokes.

One morning Gordon came back to the house calling me to report that those mean old paper carriers were shooting at our nice guys. I hurriedly dressed and went outside to protect our gang. The sky was full of streaks of light coming from the northeast quadrant of the night sky. However, no sound accompanied each streak of light. I calmed our group by explaining the fearful sight in the sky was a magnificent meteor shower, not the other gang's new weapon.

That encounter with a meteor shower was 45 years ago, and was my first. In fact, since that time I have not seen another one as strong or awesome. Last week the papers were full of reports of a meteor shower coming Wednesday morning between two and three o-clock. They called it the "Quadrantid Meteor Shower." Looking it up I found the meteors were to come from the now extinct constellation Quadrans Muralis. It is believed to have once been a hunk of rock making an orbit around our sun that became fragmented into millions of tiny pebbles. As our earth flies through the path of those pebbles, some are pulled into our atmosphere, where they reach a speed of 10,000 miles per hour. There they burn up, lighting the night sky. I decided it was time that I experience another meteor shower. Alice awakened me at 2:00 and I dressed and went to the middle of our meadow to watch the show. I saw an airplane flying so high I could not hear it. I reckoned it was from Midland going to Houston. I wondered what one would do in Houston at four in the morning. I then spotted a plane going the other way and was more puzzled at what one would do in Midland at five in the morning. A low flying plane, obviously from Georgetown, headed west, was on his way to the deer camp out around Mason. That made sense. During those three hours I stood in the middle of our meadow, turning in all directions, I saw only four small streaks of meteors. That was hardly a shower.

I think now I will encourage Gordon to get himself another paper route. Then he can call me when the sky is full of those mean old boys shooting pranks.

Made in the USA
Lexington, KY
14 May 2017